the a-z of
a   e
music

Published by
Wise Publications
14-15 Berners Street, London W1T 3LJ, UK.

Exclusive Distributors:
Music Sales Limited
Distribution Centre, Newmarket Road,
Bury St Edmunds, Suffolk IP33 3YB, UK.
Music Sales Pty Limited
120 Rothschild Avenue, Rosebery, NSW 2018, Australia.

Order No. AM91978
ISBN 0-7119-4094-0
This book © Copyright 2006 Wise Publications,
a division of Music Sales Limited.

Compiled by Nick Crispin.
Edited by Tom Farncombe.
Music arranged by David Weston,
Martin Shellard & Matt Cowe.
Music processed by Paul Ewers Music Design.

Your Guarantee of Quality

As publishers, we strive to produce every book
to the highest commercial standards.

The music has been freshly engraved and the book has
been carefully designed to minimise awkward page turns and
to make playing from it a real pleasure.

Particular care has been given to specifying
acid-free, neutral-sized paper made from pulps which
have not been elemental chlorine bleached.

This pulp is from farmed sustainable forests and
was produced with special regard for the environment.

Throughout, the printing and binding have been planned
to ensure a sturdy, attractive publication which
should give years of enjoyment.

If your copy fails to meet our high standards,
please inform us and we will gladly replace it.

This publication is not authorised for sale in
the United States of America and/or Canada

WISE PUBLICATIONS
part of The Music Sales Group
Sydney / Copenhagen / Berlin / Madrid / Tokyo

AFGHAN WHIGS: Gentlemen

Words & Music by
Gregory Dulli

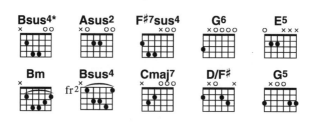

Intro

‖: Bsus⁴* Asus² | F♯7sus⁴ G⁶ | E⁵ G⁶ | G⁶ | :‖

Verse 1

          Bm   **Bsus⁴**   **Bm**
Your at - tention, please,

Bsus⁴   **Bm**   **Bsus⁴**   **G⁶**
  Now turn off the light.

F♯7sus⁴ G⁶   **Bm**   **Bsus⁴**   **Bm**
      Your in - fection, please,

Bsus⁴   **Bm**   **Bsus⁴**   **G⁶** **F♯7sus⁴**
I haven't got all night.

Chorus 1

G⁶   **Bsus⁴*** **Asus²**
Under - stand,

F♯7sus⁴ G⁶   **E⁵**   **G⁶**
     Do you under - stand?

          Bsus⁴* **Asus²**
Under - stand,

F♯7sus⁴ G⁶   **E⁵** **G⁶**
  I'm a gentle - man.

Verse 2

         Bm   **Bsus⁴**   **Bm**
I stayed in too long,

     Bsus⁴   **Bm**   **Bsus⁴**   **G⁶**
But she was the perfect fit.

F♯7sus⁴ G⁶   **Bm**   **Bsus⁴**   **Bm**
   And we dragged it out so   long this time,

Bsus⁴   **Bm**   **Bsus⁴**   **G⁶**
Started to make each other sick.

F♯7sus⁴ G⁶   **Bm Bsus⁴**   **Bm**
But now I've got time for you,

F♯7sus⁴ Bm   **Bsus⁴**   **G⁶**   **F♯7sus⁴ G⁶**
For you,   you, you,   you and me too.

Bm Bsus⁴   **Bm Bsus⁴**   **Bm Bsus⁴**
Well,   come and get it,   come and get it,

         G⁶ **F♯7sus⁴ Bm**
'Cause I'm done.

Chorus 2

G6   Bsus Asus2
Under - stand,

F#7sus4 G6   E5   G6
    Do you under - stand?

       Bsus Asus2
Under - stand,

F#7sus4 G6   E5   G6
   I'm a gentle - man, I'm a gentle - man.

Bridge

Cmaj7 D/F#   G5   Cmaj7
    I waited for the joke,

 D/F# G5   Cmaj7
It never did ar - rive.

D/F#   G5   Cmaj7
And words I thought I'd spoke.

Solo

‖: Bm Bsus4 | Bm Bsus4 | Bm Bsus4 | G6 F#7sus4 G6 :‖

Verse 3

     Bm   Bsus4
Let me in I'm cold,

Bm   Bsus4   Bm   F#7sus4
  All messed up but   no - where to go.

G6   Bm Bsus4   Bm
You got   indecision,

Bsus4   G6   F#7sus4
And indecision is my enemy.

G6   Bm Bsus4 Bm   Bsus4   Bm Bsus4
Well, un - lock the cabinet, hey,

G6   F#7sus4 G6   Bm
I'll take whatever you got.

Bsus4   Bm Bsus4   Bm
Now I'm on it,   now I'm on it,

Bsus4   G6
   And you're done.

Bridge

Cmaj7 D/F#   G5   Cmaj7
    I waited for the joke,

 D/F# G5   Cmaj7
It never did ar - rive.

D/F#   G5   Cmaj7
And words I thought I'd choke,

 D/F# G5
I hardly recognize.

Outro

‖: Cmaj7 | D/F# G5 :‖ *Play 3 times*

| Cmaj7 | Cmaj7 | Cmaj7 ‖

5

THE ASSOCIATES: Party Fears Two

Words & Music by
Billy MacKenzie & Alan Rankine

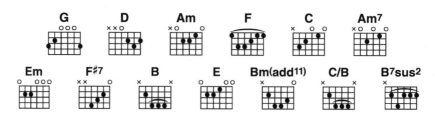

Intro

| G D | Am F | C ‖

‖: G D | Am F | C |

| Am⁷ | D | D :‖

Verse 1

       G
I'll have a shower,

           Em
And then phone my brother up.

      G
Within the hour,

          C
I'll smash an - other cup.

           D
Please don't start saying that,

        Am
Or I'll start be - lieving you.

        F♯7
If I start be - lieving you,

            B   **D**
I'll know that this party fears two.

Chorus 1

       E   **Bm(add11)**
And what if this party fears two?

        E   **Bm(add11)**
The alcohol loves you while turning you blue.

 B   **C/B**
View it from here,

       B   **C/B**
From closer to near,

     G
A - wake me.

Link 2 ‖: G D | Am F | C |

| Am7 | D | D :‖

Verse 2
        G
Don't turn a - round,
          Em
I won't have to look at you.
       G
And what's not found,
       C
Is all that I see in you.
        D
My manners are failing me,
       Am
I'm left feeling ugly.
      F♯7
And you say it's wonderful,
      B   **D**
To live with I never will.

Chorus 2   As Chorus 1

Link 3 ‖: G D | Am F | C |

| Am7 | D | D :‖

Verse 3
      G
I'm standing still,
       Em
And you say I dress too well.
      G
Still standing still,
     C
I might but it's hard to tell.
   D
Even a slight remark,
       Am
Makes nonsense and turns to shark.
   F♯7
Have I done something wrong?
       Bsus4   **B**   **D**
What's wrong's the wrong that's always in wrong.

Link 4 ‖: G D | Am F | C |

| Am7 | D | D :‖ *Repeat ad lib. to fade*

BAUHAUS: She's In Parties

Words & Music by
Daniel Ash, Kevin Haskins, Peter Murphy & David Jay

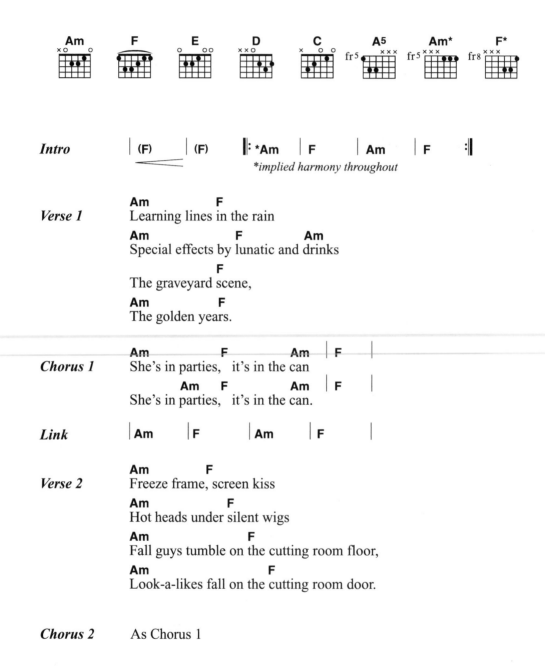

Intro | (F) | (F)   ‖: *Am | F | Am | F   :‖

implied harmony throughout

Verse 1

Am   F
Learning lines in the rain
Am   F   Am
Special effects by lunatic and drinks
                      F
The graveyard scene,
Am   F
The golden years.

Chorus 1

Am   F   Am | F |
She's in parties,   it's in the can
      Am   F   Am | F |
She's in parties,   it's in the can.

Link | Am | F | Am | F |

Verse 2

Am   F
Freeze frame, screen kiss
Am   F
Hot heads under silent wigs
Am   F
Fall guys tumble on the cutting room floor,
Am   F
Look-a-likes fall on the cutting room door.

Chorus 2   As Chorus 1

Bridge

E
Learning lines in the rain

D   C
Special effects by lunatic and drinks

E
Freeze frame, screen kiss

       D
Hot head, lights and powder

     C
It's blatantly obvious

Chorus 3   As Chorus 1

Instr. | A5 | A5 ‖: Am | F | Am | F :‖

Am*   F*
Verse 3 Hot lines under a rain of drums

Am*   F*
Cigarette props in action.

Am*   F*
Dialogue dub, now here's the rub,

Am* N.C.
She's acting her reaction.

Chorus 4   As Chorus 1

Bridge 2   As Bridge 1

Am   F   Am | F |
Chorus 5 She's in parties, it's in the can

Am   F   Am | F ‖
She's in parties, it's in the can. She's in

Outro   ‖: Am | F | Am | F :‖
      parties.   *(1° only)* She's in

      | ⌢
      | Am ‖

BECK: Loser

Words & Music by
Beck & Karl Stephenson

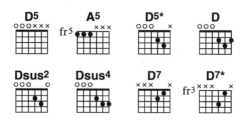

Tuning (from bottom string): D A D G B E

riff A

‖: D5* Dsus2 D Dsus2 | D5* Dsus2 D Dsus4 :‖ *Repeat as necessary*

Intro   ‖: D5   A5 | D5   A5 | D5   A5 | D5   A5 :‖

riff A
In the time of chimpanzees I was a monkey
Butane in my veins and I'm out to cut the junkie
With the plastic eyeballs, spray-paint the vegetables
Dog food stalls with the beefcake pantyhose
Kill the headlights and put it in neutral
Stock car flamin' with a loser and the cruise control
Baby's in reno with the vitamin D
Got a couple of couches, sleep on the love-seat
Someone came in sayin' I'm insane to complain
About a shotgun wedding and a stain on my shirt
Don't believe everything that you breathe
You get a parking violation and a maggot on your sleeve

    D5   **A5**
So shave your face with some mace in the dark
D5   **A5**
Savin' all your food stamps and burnin' down the trailer park
D5   **A5 D5**   **N.C.**
   Yo,   cut it.

riff A
Chorus 1   Soy un perdedor, I'm a loser baby, so why don't you kill me?
Soy un perdedor, I'm a loser baby, so why don't you kill me?

N.C. (bass only)
Verse 2   Forces of evil on a bozo nightmare
Ban all the music with a phony gas chamber
'Cuz one's got a weasel and the other's got a flag
One's on the pole, shove the other in a bag

D5   **A5**
With the rerun shows and the cocaine nose-job
D5   **A5**
  The daytime crap of the folksinger slob
D5   **A5**
  He hung himself with a guitar string
      D5   **A5**
A slab of turkey-neck and it's hangin' from a pigeon wing
D7
  You can't write if you can't relate

                                         D7*
Trade the cash for the beef for the body for the hate
        D7
And my time is a piece of wax fallin' on a termite

That's chokin' on the splinters.

Chorus 2   **riff A**
Soy un perdedor, I'm a loser baby, so why don't you kill me?
(Get crazy with the cheese whiz)
Soy un perdedor, I'm a loser baby, so why don't you kill me?
N.C.
(Drive-by body-pierce)
| **N.C.** | **N.C.** | **N.C.** | **N.C.** ‖
                        (Sooooy———)

Instr   ‖: **D5**   **A5** | **D5**   **A5** | **D5**   **A5** | **D5**   **A5** :‖

    riff A ————————————————————————
  | **D5* Dsus2 D Dsus2** | **D5* Dsus2 D Dsus4** ‖

    riff A   **N.C.**
Outro   (I'm a driver, I'm a winner; things are gonna change I can feel it)
    riff A
Soy un perdedor, I'm a loser baby, so why don't you kill me?
(I can't believe you)
Soy un perdedor, I'm a loser baby, so why don't you kill me?
Soy un perdedor, I'm a loser baby, so why don't you kill me?
(Sprechen sie deutches, baby)
Soy un perdedor, I'm a loser baby, so why don't you kill me?
                                D5
(Know what I'm sayin'?)   *Fade out*

BIG STAR: Kangaroo

Words & Music by
Alex Chilton

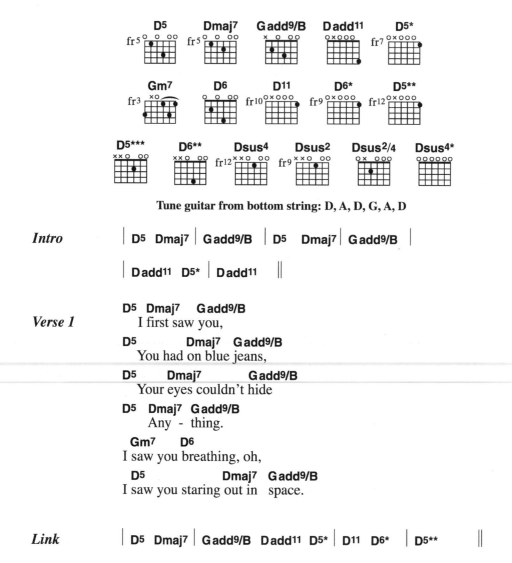

Tune guitar from bottom string: D, A, D, G, A, D

Intro | D5 Dmaj7 | Gadd9/B | D5 Dmaj7 | Gadd9/B |

| Dadd11 D5* | Dadd11 ||

Verse 1

D5 Dmaj7 Gadd9/B
I first saw you,

D5 Dmaj7 Gadd9/B
You had on blue jeans,

D5 Dmaj7 Gadd9/B
Your eyes couldn't hide

D5 Dmaj7 Gadd9/B
Any - thing.

Gm7 D6
I saw you breathing, oh,

D5 Dmaj7 Gadd9/B
I saw you staring out in   space.

Link | D5 Dmaj7 | Gadd9/B Dadd11 D5* | D11 D6* | D5** ||

Verse 2

D5   Dmaj7 Gadd9/B
I next saw   you,

D5   Dmaj7 Gadd9/B
It was at the   party,

D5   Dmaj7 Gadd9/B
Thought you was a   queen,

D5 Dmaj7 Gadd9/B
Oh so   flirty.

Gm7 D6   Gm7
I ____ came against.

Verse 3

D5   Dmaj7 Gadd9/B
Didn't say   excuse,

D5 Dmaj7   Gadd9/B
Knew what I was doing.

D5   Dmaj7 Gadd9/B
We looked very   fine

D5 Dmaj7 Gadd9/B Gm7
As we were leaving,   ooh. _____

Solo

| D5*** D6** | Dsus4 | Dsus2 D5 Dmaj7 | Gadd9/B | |
| Gadd9/B Dsus2/4 | Dsus4* | D5*** D6** | Dsus2 Dsus4 | Dsus4* ||

Verse 4

D5   Dmaj7 Gadd9/B
Like Saint   Joan,

D5   Dmaj7 Gadd9/B
Doing a cool   jerk,

D5 Dmaj7 Gadd9/B
Oh, I   want you,

D5   Dmaj7 Gadd9/B
Like a kanga - roo.

Outro

| D5 Dmaj7 | D6 | D5 Dmaj7 | D6 | |
| D5 Dmaj7 | D6 | D5 | ||

13

THE BREEDERS: Cannonball

Words & Music by
Kim Deal

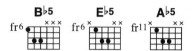

Intro   N.C (Distorted vocals, bass and drums.)

‖: B♭5 E♭5 :‖ *Play 6 times*

Verse 1

B♭5   E♭5   B♭5   E♭5
  Spit - ting in a wish - ing well
B♭5 E♭5   B♭5
  Blown to hell crash
N.C.
I'm the last splash.

‖: B♭5 E♭5 :‖ *Play 5 times*
B♭5 E♭5   B♭5   E♭5
  I know you little liber - tine
B♭5 E♭5   B♭5   E♭5
  I know you're a real coo-coo.

‖: B♭5 E♭5 :‖ *Play 4 times*

Chorus 1

B♭5   E♭5   A♭5
Want you coo-coo can - nonball,
B♭5   E♭5   A♭5
Want you coo-coo can - nonball,
B♭5   E♭5   A♭5   B♭5
  In the shade, in the shade,
        E♭5   A♭5   B♭5
  In the shade, in the shade.

‖: B♭5 E♭5 :‖ *Play 4 times*

Verse 2

B♭5 E♭5   B♭5   E♭5
  I know you little liber - tine
B♭5 E♭5   B♭5   E♭5
  I know you're a cannon - ball.

cont.

‖: B♭5 E♭5 :‖ *Play 2 times*

B♭5   E♭5   B♭5   E♭5
  I'll be your what - ever you want,

B♭5   E♭5   B♭5   N.C
  The bong in this reggae song.

Chorus 2

B♭5   E♭5   A♭5
  In the shade,

B♭5   E♭5   A♭5
  In the shade

B♭5   E♭5   A♭5   B♭5
Want you coo-coo can - nonball,

B♭5   E♭5   A♭5   B♭5
Want you coo-coo can - nonball.

Verse 3

B♭5   E♭5   B♭5   E♭5
  Spit - ting in a wish - ing well

B♭5 E♭5   B♭5
   Blown to hell, crash,

N.C.
I'm the last splash.

‖: B♭5 E♭5 :‖ *Play 2 times*

B♭5   E♭5   B♭5   E♭5
  I'll be your what - ever you want,

B♭5   E♭5   B♭5   E♭5
  The bong in this reggae song.

‖: B♭5 E♭5 :‖ *Play 4 times*

Chorus 3

B♭5   E♭5   A♭5
Want you coo-coo can - nonball,

B♭5   E♭5   A♭5
Want you coo-coo can - nonball,

B♭5   E♭5 A♭5 B♭5
  In the shade, in the shade,

B♭5   E♭5 A♭5 B♭5
  In the shade, in the shade.

Outro

‖: B♭5 E♭5 :‖ *Play 8 times*

JEFF BUCKLEY: So Real

Words & Music by
Jeff Buckley & Michael Tighe

Edim   Em   Bm/D   F#m/A   G5   C5   B(♭6)   C6

Am6   Bm7/9   Bm7   Gm6   Amadd11   D   G6sus2

Intro | N.C. | N.C. | N.C. | N.C. |

Verse 1

Edim   Em
    Love, let me sleep tonight on your couch,

| Bm/D   F#m/A | G5   C5 | B(♭6) |

Edim   Em
   And remember the smell of the fabric

Of your simple city dress.

| Bm/D   F#m/A | G5   C5 | B(♭6) |

Chorus 1

C6   Am6
   Oh... that was so real,

C6   Am6
   Oh... that was so real,

C6   Am6
   Oh... that was so real.

Instrumental | Edim | Em | Bm/D   F#m/A | G5   C5 | B(♭6) |

Verse 2

Edim   Em
   We walked around 'til the moon got full like a plate,

| Bm/D   F#m/A | G5   C5 | B(♭6) |

Edim   Em
   And the wind blew an invocation,   I fell asleep at the gate.

| Bm/D   F#m/A | G5   C5 | B(♭6) |

© Copyright 1994 Sony/ATV Songs LLC & El Viejito Music, USA.
Sony/ATV Music Publishing (UK) Limited

Verse 3

Edim   Em
And I never stepped on the cracks

'cos I thought I'd hurt my mother.

| Bm/D F♯m/A | G5 C5 | B(♭6) | |

Edim   Em
And I couldn't awake from the nightmare

That sucked me in and pulled me under,

Pulled me under…

| Bm/D F♯m/A | G5 C5 | B(♭6) | |

Chorus 2   As Chorus 1

Instrumental

| D5 | D5 | D5 | D5 |
| D5 | D5 | D5 | D♭5 |

Verse 4
(spoken)

          Edim
I love you,
Em
   But I'm afraid to love you.

| Bm/D F♯m/A | G5 C5 | B(♭6) | |

          Edim
I love you,
Em
   But I'm afraid to love you.

| Bm/D F♯m/A | G5 C5 | B(♭6) | |

I'm afraid…

Chorus 3   As Chorus 1

Coda
(w/ vocal
ad lib.)

:‖ G6sus2	Bm7/9 Bm7	Gm6 Amadd11	Gm6 Amadd11
G6sus2	Bm7/9 Bm7	Gm6	‖:
G6sus2	Bm7/9 Bm7	Gm6 Amadd11	Gm6 Amadd11
G6sus2	Bm7/9 Bm7	Gm6	N.C. D ‖

DAVID BOWIE: Be My Wife

Words & Music by
David Bowie

G7   Am   G   F   Dm   C   Em

Intro | G7 | G7 | G7 | G7 ‖

Verse 1

Am   G   F
Sometimes you get so lonely,
Am   G
Sometimes you get nowhere.
Am   G   F
I've lived all over the world,
Am   G
I've lived every place.

Link 1 ‖: Am | G F | Am | G :‖

Chorus 1

Dm   C   Dm   C
Please be mine, Stay with me,
Dm   C   Dm   Em   F   G
Share my life, Be   my wife.

Verse 2

Am   G   F | Am | G |
Sometimes you get so lonely.
Am   G   F | Am | G |
   Sometimes you get nowhere.
Am   G   F | Am | G |
I've lived all ov - er the world,
Am   G   F | Am | G |
I've lived every place.

Chorus 2   As Chorus 1

Play 6 times

Link 2 ‖: Am | G F | Am | G :‖
Sometimes you get so lone - ly.
(1° only)

Outro ‖: G | C :‖ *Repeat to fade*

CAN: I Want More

Words & Music by
Michael Karoli, Peter Gilmour, Holger Czukay, Irmin Schmidt & Jaki Leibezeit

E7   **D/E**   **E**   **D**

Intro | E⁷ D/E E⁷ D/E | E⁷ D/E E⁷ | E⁷ D/E E⁷ D/E | E⁷ D/E ‖ *cont. sim.*

Verse 1

(E⁷)
Everybody plays a game,
We don't have to say the name.
Every day come sun array,
I say good's just playing for safe.
I don't have to say no more,
You've got more time, waiting for.
Don't verify, break the law,
I want more and more and more.

Solo 1   ‖: E | D | D | E :‖ *Play 4 times*

‖: E⁷ D/E E⁷ D/E | E⁷ D/E E⁷ | E⁷ D/E E⁷ D/E | E⁷ D/E :‖ *Play 4 times*

‖: E | D | D | E :‖

Verse 2

(E⁷)
Everybody plays a game,
Voice inscription play for safe.
You've got more time, waiting for,
I want more and more and more and more,
And more and more and more and more,
And more and more and more and more,
And more and more and more and more,
And more and more and more and more, and.

Solo 2   ‖: E | D | D | E :‖ *Repeat to fade*

CAMPER VAN BEETHOVEN:
Take The Skinheads Bowling

Words & Music by
Chris Molla, David Lowery, Greg Lisher, Victor Krummenacher & Joseph Segel

Intro ‖: C | Fmaj⁷ | C | Fmaj⁷ :‖

Verse 1

C   Fmaj⁷   C | Fmaj⁷ |
Every day I get up and pray to Jah

C   Fmaj⁷   C | Fmaj⁷ |
And he increases the   number of clocks by exactly one.

C   Fmaj⁷   C | Fmaj⁷ |
Everybody's coming   home for lunch these days,

   C   Fmaj⁷   C | Fmaj⁷ |
Last night there was skinheads on my lawn.

Chorus 1

G   Fmaj⁷
Take the skinheads bowling,

      C | C |
Take them bowling.

G   Fmaj⁷
Take the skinheads bowling,

      C | C ‖
Take them bowling.

Verse 2

  C   Fmaj7   C
Some people say that bowling alley's got big lanes
      Fmaj7   C | Fmaj7 |
(Got big lanes, got big lanes)
  C   Fmaj7   C
Some people say that bowling alleys' all look the same
      Fmaj7
(Look the same, look the same)
  C   C
There's not a line that goes here that rhymes with anything
      Fmaj7
(Anything, anything)
  C   Fmaj7   C
Had a dream last night but I forget what it was
      Fmaj7
(What is was, what it was)

Chorus 2   As Chorus 1

Verse 3

  C   Fmaj7   C | Fmaj7 |
Had a dream last night about you my friend,
  C   Fmaj7   C | Fmaj7 |
Had a dream, I wanted to sleep next to plastic.
  C   Fmaj7   C | Fmaj7 |
Had a dream I wanted to lick your knees,
  C   Fmaj7   C | Fmaj7 ‖
Had a dream, it was about no - thing.

Chorus 3   As Chorus 1

Chorus 4   As Chorus 1

CAPTAIN BEEFHEART:
Big Eyed Beans From Venus

Words & Music by
Don Van Vliet

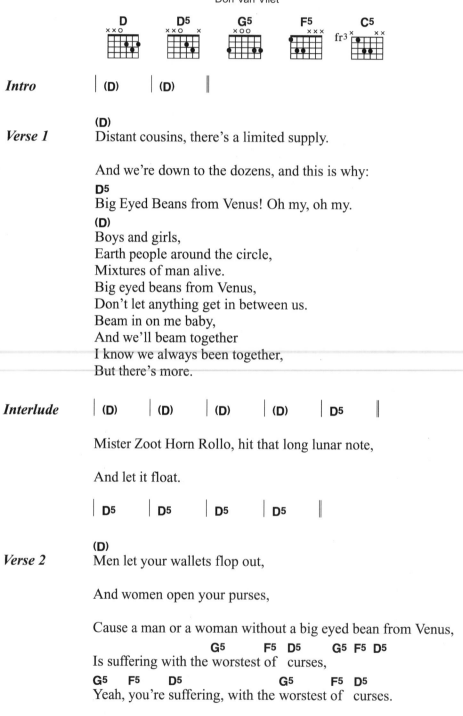

Intro　　　| (D)　　| (D)　　‖

Verse 1

(D)
Distant cousins, there's a limited supply.

And we're down to the dozens, and this is why:
D5
Big Eyed Beans from Venus! Oh my, oh my.
(D)
Boys and girls,
Earth people around the circle,
Mixtures of man alive.
Big eyed beans from Venus,
Don't let anything get in between us.
Beam in on me baby,
And we'll beam together
I know we always been together,
But there's more.

Interlude　　| (D)　　| (D)　　| (D)　　| (D)　　| D5　　‖

Mister Zoot Horn Rollo, hit that long lunar note,

And let it float.

| D5　　| D5　　| D5　　| D5　　‖

Verse 2

(D)
Men let your wallets flop out,

And women open your purses,

Cause a man or a woman without a big eyed bean from Venus,
　　　　　　　　　　　　　G5　　**F5 D5**　　**G5 F5 D5**
Is suffering with the worstest of curses,
G5　**F5**　　**D5**　　　　　　　　**G5**　　**F5 D5**
Yeah, you're suffering, with the worstest of curses.

||: **G5** **F5** | **D5** | **G5** **F5** | **D5** :||

Bridge

(D)
Put 'em out in the sun, and when the night come,

You don't have to go out and get 'em,

　　　D5　　　　　　　　　**C5**
They'll glow with you, They'll go with you,

　　　D5　　　　　　　　　**C5**
They'll show with you. Ain't no losers,

　　　　　　D5
'Cause they're on the right track,

　　　　C5
'Cause they're on the right track.

Verse 3

(D)
You can be on the right track, woman,

Of course, of course.

Ain't no SNAFU, no fol-de-rol.

Bridge 2

D5
　Check these out,
C5
　Big eyed beans from Venus.
D5
Oh, let a few out,
　　C5
Let 'em pass in between us.

Outro

(D)
Distant cousins, there's a limited supply.

And we're down to the dozens, and this is why.

Don't let anything get in between us,

Big eyed beans from Venus

Big eyed beans from Venus.

| **(D)** | **(D)** | **(D)** | **(D)** | |
| **(D)** | **(D)** | **D5** | **D5** | ||

NICK CAVE AND THE BAD SEEDS:
The Mercy Seat

Words by Nick Cave
Music by Nick Cave & Mick Harvey

Em   D5/E   Em*   D   Dm   F   C

Intro

| Em |

N.C.
It began when they come took me from my home
And put me in Death Row.
Of which I am nearly wholly innocent, you know.
And I'll say it again

Em
I am not afraid to die.

Verse 1

Em   D5/E   Em   D5/E   Em
I began to warm and chill to   objects and their fields.
                D5/E   Em   D5/E   Em
A ragged cup, a twisted mop, the face of Jesus in my soup.
                  D5/E   Em   D5/E
Those sinister dinner deals,   the meal trolley's wicked wheels.
        Em   D5/E   Em   D5/E   Em
A hooked bone rising from my food, all things either good or ungood.

Chorus 1

Em   Em*   D
And the mercy seat is waiting,   And I think my head is burning,
                              Dm   F
And in a way I'm yearning, To be done with all this measuring of proof.

An eye for an eye and a tooth for a tooth,
                    C   Em
And anyway I told the truth and I'm not afraid to die.

Verse 2

	Em	D5/E		Em		D5/E	Em

Interpret signs and cata - logue, a blackened tooth, a scarlet fog.

          D5/E   **Em**
The walls are bad, black bottom kind.

          D5/E   **Em**
They are sick breath at my hind.

          D5/E   **Em**
They are sick breath at my hind.

          D5/E
They are sick breath at my hind.

     Em   **D5/E** **Em** **D5/E**
They are sick breath gathering at my hind.

Chorus 2

 Em   **Em***
I hear stories from the chamber,

                           D
How Christ was born into a manger.

                       Dm
And like some ragged stranger died upon the cross.

                                F
And might I say it seems so fitting in its way,

                 C
He was a carpenter by trade or at least that's what I'm told.

Verse 3

 Em **D5/E**   **Em**   **D5/E**   **Em**
Like my good hand, tattooed evil across it's brother's fist.

          D5/E   **Em**   **D5/E**
That filthy five! They did nothing to challenge or resist.

Chorus 3

 Em   **Em***
In Heaven His throne is made of gold,

                         D
The ark of his Testament is stowed.

                        Dm
A throne from which I'm told all history does unfold.

         F
Down here it's made of wood and wire,

                     C   **Em**
And my body is on fire and   God is never far a - way.

Chorus 4

 Em   **Em***
Into the mercy seat I climb,

                      D
My head is shaved, my head is wired.

                     Dm
And like the moth that tries to enter the bright eye,

          F   C

So I go shuffling out of life, just to hide in death awhile.

                        Em

And anyway I never lied.

Verse 4

   Em   D5/E   Em

My kill-hand is called Evil,

                 D5/E   Em

Wears a wedding band that's Good.

           D5/E   Em

'Tis a long-suffering shackle,

           D5/E

Collaring all that rebel blood.

Chorus 5

   Em   Em*

And the mercy seat is burning,

                              D

And I think my head is glowing.

And in a way I'm hoping

         Dm   F

To be done with all this weighing up of truth.

An eye for an eye and a tooth for a tooth,

                    C

And I've got nothing left to lose,

                    Em

And I'm not afraid to die.

Chorus 6

   Em   Em*

And the mercy seat is waiting,

                              D

And I think my head is burning.

And in a way I'm yearning

         Dm   F

To be done with all this measuring of proof.

An eye for an eye and a tooth for a tooth,

                    C

And anyway there was no proof,

                  Em

And nor a motive why.

Chorus 7

   Em   **Em***   **D**

And the mercy seat is waiting,   And I think my head is burning.

                              Dm

And in a way I'm yearning, To be done with all this measuring of proof.

                         F   **C**

A life for a life and a truth for a truth, And anyway there was no proof,

                 Em

And I'm not afraid to die.

Chorus 8

   Em   **Em***   **D**

And the mercy seat is waiting,   And I think my head is smoking.

                              Dm

And in a way I'm hoping, To be done with all this looks of dis - belief.

                         F   **C**

An eye for an eye and a tooth for a tooth, And anyway I told the truth,

                 Em

And I'm not afraid to die.

Chorus 9

   Em   **Em***   **D**

And the mercy seat is waiting,   And I think my head is burning.

                              Dm

And in a way I'm yearning, To be done with all this measuring of proof.

                         F   **C**

An eye for an eye and a truth for a truth, And anyway I told the truth,

                 Em

And I'm not afraid to die.

Chorus 10

   Em   **Em***   **D**

And the mercy seat is waiting,   And I think my head is burning.

                              Dm

And in a way I'm yearning, To be done with all this measuring of proof.

                         F   **C**

An eye for an eye and a truth for a truth, And anyway I told the truth,

                 Em

And I'm not afraid to die.

Chorus 11

   Em   **Em***   **D**

And the mercy seat is waiting, And I think my head is burning.

                              Dm

And in a way I'm yearning, To be done with all this measuring of proof.

                         F   **C**

An eye for an eye and a tooth for a tooth, And anyway I told the truth,

                 Em

I'm afraid I told a lie.

Outro   ‖: **Em** | **Em*** | **D** | **Dm** |

                | **Dm** | **F** | **C**   :‖ *Repeat to fade*

THE CHURCH: Under The Milky Way

Words & Music by
Steven Kilberg & Karin Jansson

Am	Asus4	Fmaj7	G	F#m7♭5	Em7	C

Intro ‖: Am Asus4 | Fmaj7 G :‖

Verse 1

Am   Asus4   Fmaj7 G
Sometimes when this place gets kind of empty,

Am   Asus4   Fmaj7 G
Sound of their breath fades with the light.

Am   Asus4 Fmaj7   G
I think about   the loveless fascina - tion,

Am   Asus4   Fmaj7 G
Under the Milky Way to - night.

Am   F#m7♭5   Fmaj7   Em7
Lower the curtain down in Memphis,

Am   F#m7♭5   Fmaj7 Em7
Lower the curtain down all right.

Am   F#m7♭5 Fmaj7   Em7
I got no time for private consul - tation,

Am   F#m7♭5   Fmaj7 Em7
Under the Milky Way to - night.

Pre chorus 1

G   Fmaj7
Wish I knew what you were looking for.

G   Fmaj7
Might have known what you would find.

Chorus 1

Am F#m7♭5   Fmaj7 Em7
And it's something quite pe - culiar,

Am   F#m7♭5   Fmaj7 Em7
Something shimmering and white.

Am   F#m7♭5   Fmaj7   Em7
It leads you here, des - pite your desti - nation,

Am   F#m7♭5   Fmaj7 Em7
Under the Milky Way to - night.

Pre chorus 2

```
        G                         Fmaj7
        Wish I knew what you were looking for.
        G                                Fmaj7
        Might have known what you would find.
        G                         Fmaj7
        Wish I knew what you were looking for.
        G                                Fmaj7
        Might have known what you would find.
```

Solo 1

‖: C   G ‖ C   G ‖ Am   ‖ Am   :‖   *Play 4 times*

Chorus 2

```
        Am        F♯m7♭5              Fmaj7  Em7
        And it's something quite pe - culiar,
        Am              F♯m7♭5        Fmaj7  Em7
        Something shimmering and white.
        Am              F♯m7♭5      Fmaj7        Em7
        It leads you here,    des - pite your desti - nation,
        Am              F♯m7♭5      Fmaj7  Em7
        Under the Milky Way to - night.
```

Pre chorus 3

```
        G                         Fmaj7
        Wish I knew what you were looking for.
        G                                Fmaj7
        Might have known what you would find.
        G                         Fmaj7
        Wish I knew what you were looking for.
        G                                Fmaj7
        Might have known what you would find.
```

Link

‖ Am F♯m7♭5 ‖ Fmaj7 Em7 ‖ Am F♯m7♭5 ‖

```
        Am        F♯m7♭5      Fmaj7  Em7
        Under the Milky Way to - night.
        Am        F♯m7♭5      Fmaj7  Em7
        Under the Milky Way to - night.
        Am        F♯m7♭5      Fmaj7  Em7
        Under the Milky Way to - night.
```

Repeat to fade

Outro

‖: Am F♯m7♭5 ‖ Fmaj7 Em7 ‖ Am F♯m7♭5 ‖ Fmaj7 Em7 :‖

THE CLASH: Complete Control

Words & Music by
Mick Jones & Joe Strummer

E   B   C#m   A   G   D   Bm

fr7   fr7   fr4   fr5   fr3   fr10   fr7

Intro   ‖: E | E | E | E   :‖

Verse 1

    E
They said release 'Remote Control'
    B   E
But we didn't want it on the label.

They said, fly to Amsterdam,
    B   E
The people laughed but the press went mad.
C#m   A B   E
Ooh ooh ooh someone's really smart,
C#m   A   B
Ooh ooh ooh com - plete control, that's a laugh.

Verse 2

        E
On the last tour my mates couldn't get in,
    B   E
I'd open up the back door but they'd get run out again.

At every hotel we was met by the law,
B   E
Come for the party - come to make sure!
C#m   A   B   E
Ooh ooh ooh have we done something wrong?
C#m   A   B
Ooh ooh ooh com - plete control, even over this song.

Solo | E | E | B | E | E | E | B | E |

| C#m | A | G | G | C#m | A | E | E   ‖
You're my guitar hero!

Verse 3

    E
They said we'd be artistically free
B   E
When we signed that bit of paper.

They meant let's make a lotsa mon-ee
```
      B
```
An' worry about it later.
```
C♯m     A   B                    E
```
Ooh ooh ooh I'll never under - stand,
```
C♯m     A       B
```
Ooh ooh ooh com - plete control - lemme see your other hand!


```
      B         A          C♯m
```
Bridge   I don't trust you,
```
                              D     A
```
Why do you trust me?
```
E
```
Huh?
```
B               A           C♯m
```
All over the news spread fast,
```
          D           A
```
They're dirty, they're filthy.
```
                          E
```
They ain't gonna last!
```
B               A       C♯m
```
This is Joe Public speaking,
```
            D           A                    E
```
I'm con - trolled in the body,   controlled in the mind.
```
B               A           C♯m
```
This is the Punk Rockers,
```
              D             A               E
```
We're con - trolled in the body,   controlled in the mind.


```
      B    A   C♯m
```
Outro   Total,
```
D      A        E
```
C-o-n— con - trol.
```
Bm  A   C♯m
```
  Total,   they want control.
```
D      A        E
```
C-o-n— con - trol.


```
Bm   A   C♯m
```


```
D      A        E
```
C-o-n— con - trol, that means you!


```
Bm   A   C♯m
```


```
D      A        E
```
C-o-n— con - trol.

THE COCTEAU TWINS:
Pearly Dewdrops' Drops

Words & Music by
Elizabeth Fraser, Simon Raymonde & Robin Guthrie

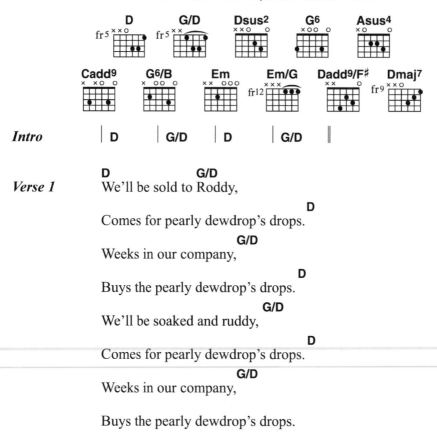

Intro | D | G/D | D | G/D   ‖

Verse 1

D   G/D
We'll be sold to Roddy,

                                      D
Comes for pearly dewdrop's drops.

                          G/D
Weeks in our company,

                              D
Buys the pearly dewdrop's drops.

                          G/D
We'll be soaked and ruddy,

                                      D
Comes for pearly dewdrop's drops.

                          G/D
Weeks in our company,

Buys the pearly dewdrop's drops.

Chorus 1

Dsus2   G6
We'll be soaked when Roddy comes,

            Asus4
Rows of pearly dewdrop's drops.

            Cadd9
'Tis the lucky, lucky penny, penny, penny

G6/B
Buys the pearly dew drips soaks.

Dsus2   G6
We'll be soaked when Roddy comes,

            Asus4
Rows of pearly dewdrop's drops.

            Cadd9
'Tis the lucky, lucky penny, penny, penny

                              (D)
Buys the pearly dew drips soaks.

Verse 2

    D   **G/D**
Taciturn to fellow,

                          D
So try to turn to loan him these.

                    G/D
Bruised your eye on her staff,

                          D
So when he turned around he saw.

           G/D
Taciturn to fellow,

                          D
So try to turn to loan him these.

                    G/D
Bruised your eye on her staff,

                      (Dsus2)
So when he turned around he saw.

Chorus 2

Dsus2   **G6**
We'll be soaked when Roddy comes,

          Asus4
Rows of pearly dewdrop's drops.

          Cadd9
'Tis the lucky, lucky penny, penny, penny

G6/B   **(D)**
Buys the pearly dew drips soaks.

Dsus2   **G6**
We'll be soaked when Roddy comes,

          Asus4
Rows of pearly dewdrop's drops.

          Cadd9
'Tis the lucky, lucky penny, penny, penny

G6/B
Buys the pearly dew drips.

Bridge

| **Em** | **Em/G** | **Dadd9/F♯** | **Dmaj7** | **Em** | **Em/G** |
Oh._____

Chorus 3   As Chorus 1

Chorus 4

   Dsus2   **G6**
‖: We'll be sold to Roddy, sold to Roddy,

          Asus4
Rows of pearly dewdrop's drops.

          Cadd9
'Tis the lucky, lucky penny, penny, penny

G6/B
Buys the pearly dew drips soaks. :‖ *Play 3 times then fade*

CRASS: Big A, Little A

Words & Music by
Steve Ignorant, Eve Libertine, De-Vivre, Hari Nana, Phil Free, Pete Wright, Penny Rimbaud & Ge Sus

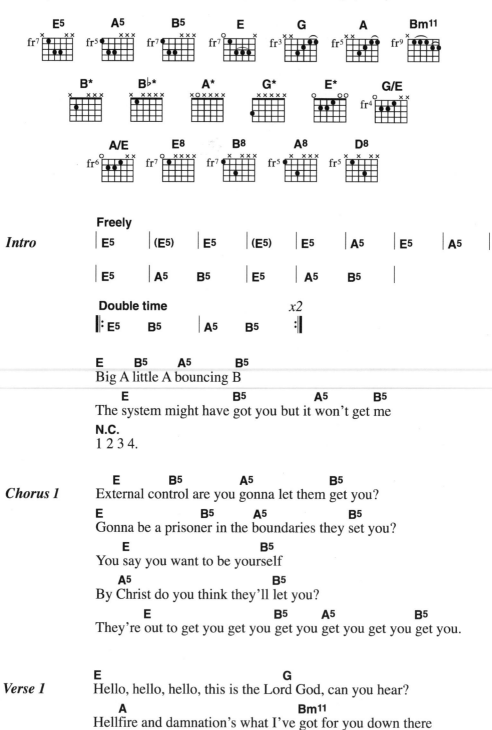

Intro

Freely

| E5 | (E5) | E5 | (E5) | E5 | A5 | E5 | A5 | |

| E5 | A5 B5 | E5 | A5 B5 | |

Double time   *x2*

‖: E5 B5 | A5 B5 :‖

```
E      B5      A5        B5
Big A little A bouncing B
        E              B5          A5        B5
The system might have got you but it won't get me
N.C.
1 2 3 4.
```

Chorus 1
```
        E      B5      A5          B5
External control are you gonna let them get you?
E              B5      A5              B5
Gonna be a prisoner in the boundaries they set you?
        E              B5
You say you want to be yourself
    A5                      B5
By Christ do you think they'll let you?
            E              B5      A5          B5
They're out to get you get you get you get you get you get you.
```

Verse 1
```
    E                              G
Hello, hello, hello, this is the Lord God, can you hear?
        A                          Bm11
Hellfire and damnation's what I've got for you down there
```

<pre>
      E   G
On Earth I have ambassadors, archbishop, vicar, post
      A   Bm11
We'll blind you with morality, you'd best abandon any hope,
          E   G
We're telling you you'd better pray 'cause you were born in sin
          A   Bm11
Right from the start we'll build a cell and then we'll lock you in
          E   G
We sit in holy judgement condemning those that stray
          A   Bm11
We offer our forgiveness, but first we'll make you pay.
</pre>

Chorus 2
<pre>
          E   B5   A5   B5
External control are you gonna let them get you?
E   B5   A5   B5
Gonna be a prisoner in the boundaries they set you?
          E   B5
You say you want to be yourself
          A5   B5
By Christ do you think they'll let you?
              E   B5   A5   B5
They're out to get you get you get you get you get you get you.
</pre>

Verse 2
<pre>
      E   G
Hello, hello, hello, now here's a message from your Queen
          A   Bm11
As figurehead of the status quo I set the social scene
          E   G
I'm most concerned about my people, I want to give them peace
              A   Bm11
So I'm making sure they stay in line with my army and police.
          E   G
My prisons and my mental homes have ever open doors
          A   Bm11
For those amongst my subjects who dare to ask for more
          E   G
Unrulyness and disrespect are things I can't allow
              A   Bm11
So I'll see the peasants grovel if they refuse to bow.
</pre>

Chorus 3   As Chorus 1

Verse 3
<pre>
          E   G
Introducing the Prime Sinister, she's a mother to us all
          A   Bm11
Like the Dutch boy's finger in the dyke her arse is in the wall
</pre>

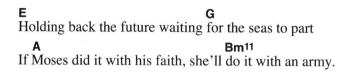

```
E                              G
Holding back the future waiting for the seas to part
  A                              Bm11
If Moses did it with his faith, she'll do it with an army.
```

Bridge

```
N.C.   B*                                    B♭*  A*   G*
Who at times of threatened crisis are certain to be there
B*                              B♭*   A*    G*
Guarding national heritage no matter what or where
B*                              B♭*    A*
Palaces for kings and queens, mansions for the rich
G*    B*                        B♭*  A*
   Protection for the wealthy, defence of privilege
G*         B*                            B♭*  A*
   They've learnt the ropes in Ireland, engaged in civil war
G*       B*                           B♭*      A*
Fighting for the ruling classes in their battle against the poor.
G*    B*                          B♭*      A*
   So Ireland's just an island? It's an island    of the mind
G*       B*                              B♭*    A*
   Great Britain? Future? Bollocks, you'd better look behind.
Em/G    E
   Round every other corner stands P.C. 1984
```

```
Guardian of the future, he'll implement the law
     G/E
He's there as a grim reminder that no matter what you do

Big brother's system's always there with his beady eyes on you.
     A/E
From God to local bobby, in home and street and school

They've got your name and number while you've just got their rule
     E5
We've got to look for methods to undermine those powers

It's time to change the tables. The future must be ours!
```

Instrumental

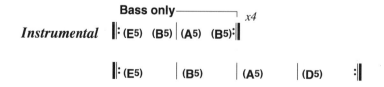

Verse 4

  (E5)   **(B5)**   **(A5)**   **(E5)**
  Be exactly who you want to be, do what you want to do
    (B5)   **(A5)**   **(D5)**
I am he and she is she but you're the only you.
     (B5)   **(A5)**   **(D5)**
No one else has got your eyes, can see the things you see
(E5)   **(B5)**   **(A5)**   **(E5)**
 It's up to you to change your life and my life's up to me
      (B5)   **(A5)**   **(D5)**
The problems that you suffer from, are problems that you make
     (B5)   **(A5)**   **(E5)**
The shit we have to climb through is the shit we choose to take.
     (B5)   **(A5)**   **(D5)**
If you don't like the life you live, change it now it's yours
    (B5)   **(A5)**   **(E5)**
Nothing has effect if you don't recognise the cause.
    (E5)   **(B5)**   **(A5)**   **(D5)**
If the programme's not the one you want, get up, turn off the set
    (B5)   **(A5)**   **(E5)**
It's only you that can decide what life you're gonna get
    (B5)   **(A5)** **(E5)**
If you don't like religion you can be the antichrist
    (B5)   **N.C.**
If you're tired of politics you can be an anarchist.

But no one ever changed the church by pulling down a steeple

You'll never change the system by bombing Number Ten

Systems just aren't made of bricks they're mostly made of people

You may send them into hiding, but they'll be back again.
     (B5)   **(A5)**   **(E5)**
If you don't like the rules they make, refuse to play their game
     (B5)   **(A5)**   **(D5)**
If you don't want to be a number, don't give them your name
     (B5)   **(A5)**   **(D5)**
If you don't want to be caught out, refuse to hear their question
    (B5)   **(A5)**   **(E5)**
Silence is a virtue, use it for your own protection.
       (B5)   **(A5)**   **(D5)**
They'll try to make you play their game, refuse to show your face
      (B5)   **(A5)**   **(E5)**
If you don't want to be beaten down, refuse to join their race
     (B5)   **(A5)**   **(D5)**
Be exactly who you want to be, do what you want to do
    (B5)   **(A5)**   **(E5)**
I am he and she is she but you're the only you.

Outro   ‖: E8 | B8 | A8 | D8 :‖ *Repeat to fade*

THE CURE: A Forest

Words & Music by
Simon Gallup, Laurence Tolhurst, Matthieu Hartley & Robert Smith

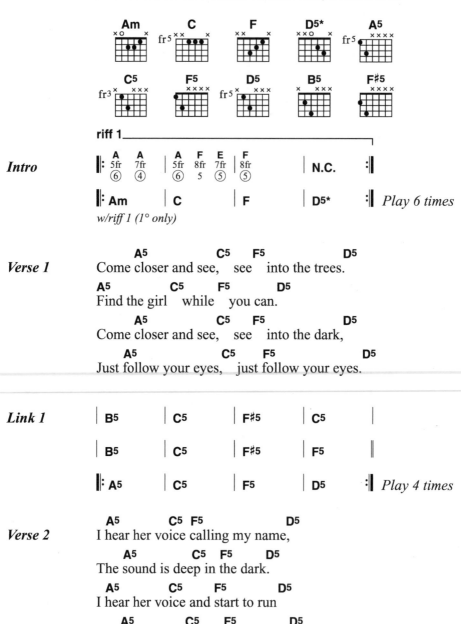

Intro

```
riff 1
┌────────────────────────────────────┐
║: A    A  │ A    F    E  │ F    │      N.C.      :║
   5fr  7fr│ 5fr  8fr  7fr│ 8fr  │
   ⑥    ④ │ ⑥    5    ⑤ │ ⑤   │
```

║: Am   │ C   │ F   │ D5*   :║   *Play 6 times*

w/riff 1 (1° only)

Verse 1

```
      A5              C5    F5            D5
Come closer and see,  see   into the trees.
A5            C5      F5      D5
Find the girl   while   you can.
      A5              C5    F5            D5
Come closer and see,   see   into the dark,
      A5                   C5    F5              D5
Just follow your eyes,    just follow your eyes.
```

Link 1

```
│ B5     │ C5     │ F#5    │ C5     │
│ B5     │ C5     │ F#5    │ F5     ║
║: A5    │ C5     │ F5     │ D5     :║   Play 4 times
```

Verse 2

```
      A5          C5  F5          D5
I hear her voice calling my name,
      A5            C5  F5      D5
The sound is deep in the dark.
      A5          C5      F5         D5
I hear her voice and start to run
      A5            C5      F5          D5
Into   the trees,   in - to the trees.
```

Link 2

| B5 | C5 | F♯5 | C5 | |

| B5 | C5 | F♯5 | F5 | |

| A5 | C5 | F5 | D5 ‖

Into the trees.

‖: A5 | C5 | F5 | D5 :‖ *Play 3 times*

Verse 3

    A5   C5   F5   D5
Sud - denly I stop,   but I know it's too late
    A5   C5   F5 D5
I'm lost in a for - est, all a - lone.
    A5   C5   F5   D5
The girl was never there, it's al - ways the same,
    A5   C5
I'm running towards nothing.
F5   D5
Again and again and again and again and
    B5   C5
A - gain and again and again and again and
    F♯5   C5   B5   C5 | A♯5 | F5 |
A - gain and again and again and a - gain and a - gain.

Outro

‖: A5 | C5 | F5 | D5 :‖ *Play 16 times*
  w/ad lib. gtr.

39

DINOSAUR JR: Freak Scene

Words & Music by
Joseph Mascis

D   Em   A*   A6   A   E5

Aadd9   E5*   F#11   F#5   D*   E   D5

Intro | D | Em | A* | A6 A* ‖

Verse 1

D   Em
Seen enough to eye you

A
But I've seen too much to try you

D   Em
It's always weirdness while you

A
Dig it much too much to fry you.

D   Em
The weirdness flows between us

A
Anyone can tell to see us

D   Em
Freak scene just can't believe us

A
Why can't it just be cool and free us?

Link 1 | D | D | D | D   ‖

‖: E5 | E5 | Aadd9 | Aadd9 :‖ *Play 4 times*

Verse 2

E5*
Seen enough to eye you

F♯11
But I've seen too much to try you

E5*
It's always weirdness while you

F♯11
Dig it much too much to fry you.

E5*
The weirdness flows between us

F♯11
Anyone can tell to see us

E5*
Freak scene just can't believe us

F♯11
Can't it just be cool and leave us?

Link 2 | **F♯5** | **F♯5**   ‖

Verse 3

D*   **Em**
It's so fucked I can't believe it,

Aadd9
If there's a way I wish we'd see it

D*   **Em**
How could it work, just can't conceive it

Aadd9
Oh what a mess it's just to leave it.

Solo ‖: **D*** | **E** | **Aadd9** | **Aadd9** :‖ *Play 6 times*

Verse 4

D*   **Em**
Sometimes I don't thrill you

Aadd9
Sometimes I think I'll kill you,

D*   **Em**
Just don't let me fuck up will you?

Aadd9
'Cause when I need a friend it's still you.

Outro ‖: **D*** | **Em** | **Aadd9** | **Aadd9** :‖ *Play 6 times*
(1° only) What a mess.

| **D5**   ‖

DEAD KENNEDYS: Holiday In Cambodia

Words & Music by
Jello Biafra, Klaüs Fluoride, East Bay Ray & Bruce Slesinger

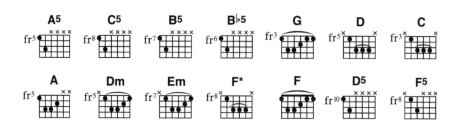

Intro   25" of guitar noise . . .

fade in on A5

                             x17

‖: **C5** **B5** **B♭5** | **A5**   :‖

            C5   **B5**   **B♭5** **A5**

Verse 1   So you been to school for a year or two
            C5   **B5** **B♭5** **A5**
And you know you've seen it all
    C5   **B5** **B♭5**   **A5**
In daddy's car thinking you'll go far
          C5   **B5** **B♭5** **A5**
Back east your type don't crawl.

         G   **D**
Play ethnicky jazz to parade your snazz
         G   **D**
On your five grand stereo
G   **D**
Braggin' that you know how the niggers feel the cold
         G   **D**
And the slums got so much soul.

            C   **G** **C** **A**
It's time to taste what you fear most
D   **C**   **G** **C** **A**
Right Guard will not help you here
Dm   **Em**   **F*** **Em**
Brace yourself, my dear…
Dm   **Em**   **F*** **Em**
Brace yourself, my dear…

Chorus 1

      A   **C** **D**
It's a holiday in Cambodia

C **A**   **C** **D**
It's tough kid, but it's life

C **A**   **C** **D**
It's a holiday in Cambodia

C   **A**   **(C) F**
Don't forget to pack a wife.

Instrumental

                             x4
‖: **C5** **B5** **B♭5** | **A5**   :‖

Verse 2

          C5   **B5**
You're a star-belly sneech,

B♭5 **A5**
You suck like a leech

       C5   **B5**   **B♭5 A5**
You want everyone to act like you

     C5   **B5**   **B♭5**   **A5**
Kiss ass while you bitch so you   can get rich

        C5   **B5**   **B♭5 A5**
While your boss gets richer off you.

   G   **D**
Well you'll work harder with a gun in your back

     G   **D**
For a bowl of rice a day

G   **D**
Slave for soldiers 'til you starve

       G   **D**
Then your head is skewered on a stake.

         C   **G**   **C A**
But now you can go where the people are one

D   **C**   **G C**   **A**
Now you can go where they get things done

Dm   **Em**   **F* Em**
What you need, my son . . .

Dm   **Em**   **F* Em**
What you need, my son . . .

Chorus 2

      A   **C** **D**
Is a holiday in Cambodia

C   **A**   **C D**
Where people dress in black

C **A**   **C** **D**
  A holiday in Cambodia

C   **A**   **C F**
Where you'll kiss ass or crack.

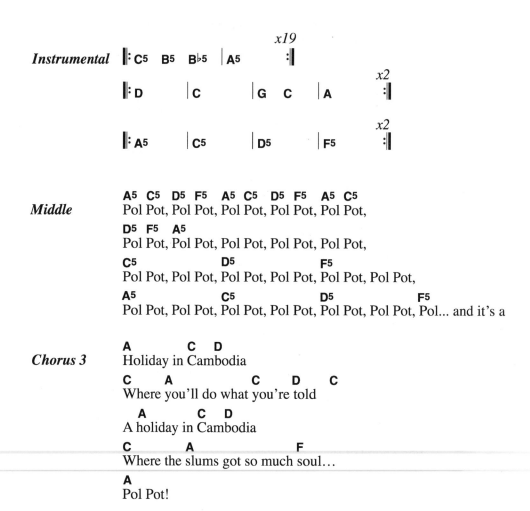

Instrumental

‖: C5 B5 B♭5 | A5 :‖ *x19*

‖: D | C | G C | A :‖ *x2*

‖: A5 | C5 | D5 | F5 :‖ *x2*

Middle

A5 C5 D5 F5 A5 C5 D5 F5 A5 C5
Pol Pot, Pol Pot, Pol Pot, Pol Pot, Pol Pot,

D5 F5 A5
Pol Pot, Pol Pot, Pol Pot, Pol Pot, Pol Pot,

C5   D5   F5
Pol Pot, Pol Pot, Pol Pot, Pol Pot, Pol Pot, Pol Pot,

A5   C5   D5   F5
Pol Pot, Pol Pot, Pol Pot, Pol Pot, Pol Pot, Pol Pot, Pol... and it's a

Chorus 3

A   C D
Holiday in Cambodia

C   A   C   D   C
Where you'll do what you're told

A   C D
A holiday in Cambodia

C   A   F
Where the slums got so much soul…

A
Pol Pot!

44

NICK DRAKE: Pink Moon

Words & Music by
Nick Drake

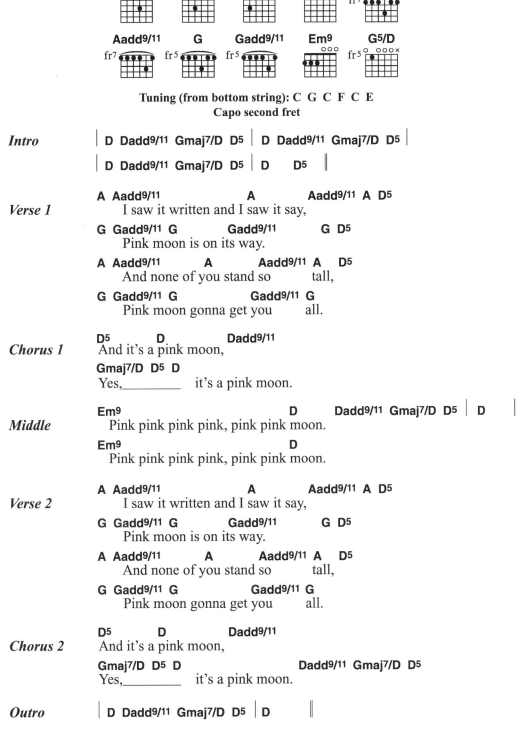

Tuning (from bottom string): C G C F C E
Capo second fret

Intro | D Dadd9/11 Gmaj7/D D5 | D Dadd9/11 Gmaj7/D D5 |

| D Dadd9/11 Gmaj7/D D5 | D   D5 ||

Verse 1
A Aadd9/11   A   Aadd9/11 A D5
   I saw it written and I saw it say,
G Gadd9/11 G   Gadd9/11   G D5
   Pink moon is on its way.
A Aadd9/11   A   Aadd9/11 A   D5
   And none of you stand so   tall,
G Gadd9/11 G   Gadd9/11 G
   Pink moon gonna get you   all.

Chorus 1
D5   D   Dadd9/11
And it's a pink moon,
Gmaj7/D D5 D
Yes,_____ it's a pink moon.

Middle
Em9   D   Dadd9/11 Gmaj7/D D5 | D |
   Pink pink pink pink, pink pink moon.
Em9   D
   Pink pink pink pink, pink pink moon.

Verse 2
A Aadd9/11   A   Aadd9/11 A D5
   I saw it written and I saw it say,
G Gadd9/11 G   Gadd9/11   G D5
   Pink moon is on its way.
A Aadd9/11   A   Aadd9/11 A   D5
   And none of you stand so   tall,
G Gadd9/11 G   Gadd9/11 G
   Pink moon gonna get you   all.

Chorus 2
D5   D   Dadd9/11
And it's a pink moon,
Gmaj7/D D5 D   Dadd9/11 Gmaj7/D D5
Yes,_____ it's a pink moon.

Outro | D Dadd9/11 Gmaj7/D D5 | D ||

THE ELECTRIC PRUNES:
I Had Too Much To Dream (Last Night)

Words & Music by
Annette Tucker & Nancie Mantz

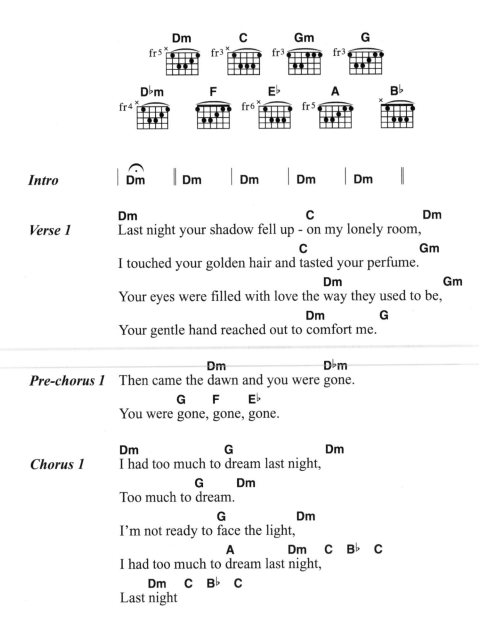

Intro
| Dm || Dm | Dm | Dm | Dm ||

Verse 1
Dm   C   Dm
Last night your shadow fell up - on my lonely room,
                        C   Gm
I touched your golden hair and tasted your perfume.
                        Dm   Gm
Your eyes were filled with love the way they used to be,
                    Dm   G
Your gentle hand reached out to comfort me.

Pre-chorus 1
                 Dm   D♭m
Then came the dawn and you were gone.
          G   F   E♭
You were gone, gone, gone.

Chorus 1
Dm   G   Dm
I had too much to dream last night,
          G   Dm
Too much to dream.
          G   Dm
I'm not ready to face the light,
             A   Dm C B♭ C
I had too much to dream last night,
      Dm C B♭ C
Last night

Verse 2

  Dm   **C**   **Dm**
  The room was empty as I staggered from my bed,

           C   **Gm**
  I could not bear the image racing through my head.

         Dm   **Gm**
  You were so real that I could feel your eagerness,

            Dm   **G**
  And when you raised your lips for me to kiss.

Pre-chorus 2

      Dm   **D♭m**
  Came the dawn and you were gone,

    G   **F** **E♭**
  You were gone, gone, gone.

Chorus 2

  Dm   **G**   **Dm**
  ‖: I had too much to dream last night,

      G **Dm**
  Too much to dream.

       G   **Dm**
  I'm not ready to face the light,

        A   **Dm** **C** **B♭** **C**
  I had too much to dream last night,

    Dm **C** **B♭** **C**
  Last night.   :‖

Outro

  (C)   **Dm** **C** **B♭**
  ‖: Oh, too much to dream.

  C   **Dm** **C** **B♭**
  Oh, too much to dream.

  C   **Dm**   **C** **B♭**
  Too much to dream last night.

  C   **Dm** **C** **B♭**
  Oh, too much to dream. :‖ *Repeat to fade*

BRIAN ENO: Needle In The Camel's Eye

Words & Music by
Phil Manzanera & Brian Eno

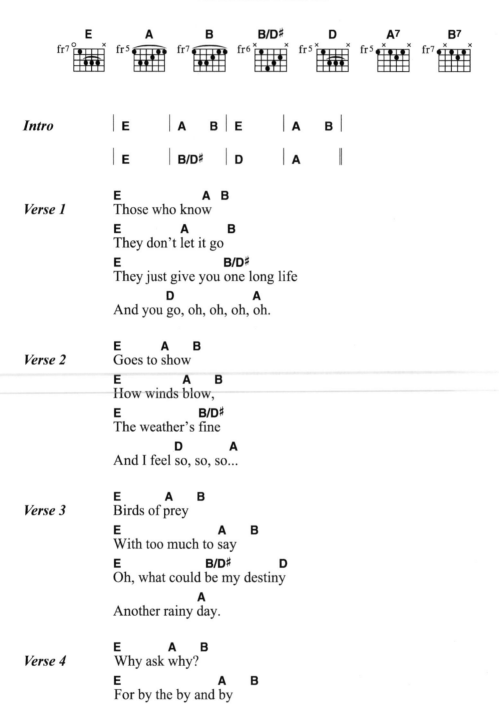

Intro

| E | A   B | E | A   B |
| E | B/D♯ | D | A ‖

Verse 1

E   A B
Those who know

E   A   B
They don't let it go

E   B/D♯
They just give you one long life

         D   A
And you go, oh, oh, oh, oh.

Verse 2

E   A   B
Goes to show

E   A   B
How winds blow,

E   B/D♯
The weather's fine

         D   A
And I feel so, so, so...

Verse 3

E   A   B
Birds of prey

E   A   B
With too much to say

E   B/D♯   D
Oh, what could be my destiny

         A
Another rainy day.

Verse 4

E   A   B
Why ask why?

E   A   B
For by the by and by

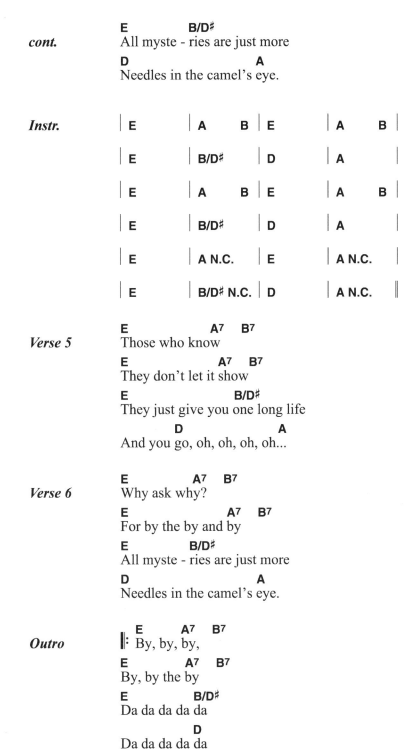

cont.

E   B/D♯
All myste - ries are just more
D   A
Needles in the camel's eye.

Instr.

E	A B	E	A B
E	B/D♯	D	A
E	A B	E	A B
E	B/D♯	D	A
E	A N.C.	E	A N.C.
E	B/D♯ N.C.	D	A N.C.

Verse 5

E   A7 B7
Those who know
E   A7 B7
They don't let it show
E   B/D♯
They just give you one long life
    D   A
And you go, oh, oh, oh, oh...

Verse 6

E   A7 B7
Why ask why?
E   A7 B7
For by the by and by
E   B/D♯
All myste - ries are just more
D   A
Needles in the camel's eye.

Outro

‖: E A7 B7
By, by, by,
E   A7 B7
By, by the by
E   B/D♯
Da da da da da
    D
Da da da da da
    A
Da da da da da... :‖ *Repeat to fade*

FAITH NO MORE: We Care A Lot

Words & Music by
Mike Bordin, Roddy Bottum, Bill Gould & Charles Mosley

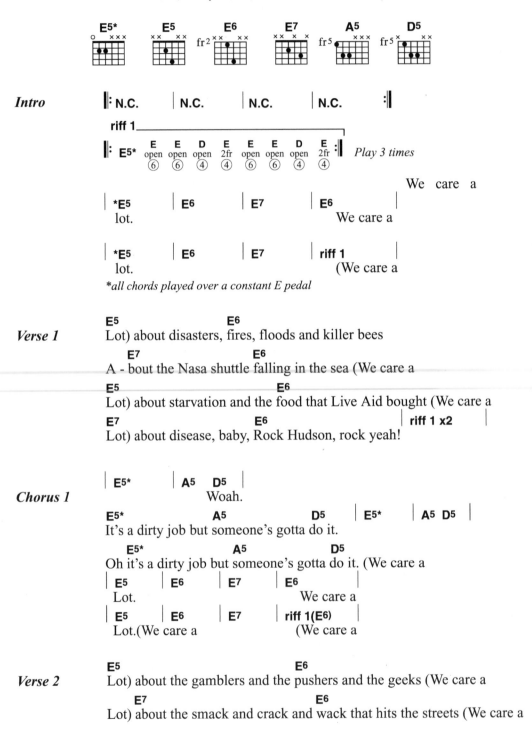

Intro ‖: N.C. | N.C. | N.C. | N.C. :‖

riff 1

‖: E5* E E D E E E D E :‖ *Play 3 times*
open open open 2fr open open open 2fr
⑥ ⑥ ④ ④ ⑥ ⑥ ④ ④

We care a

| *E5 | E6 | E7 | E6 |
lot.   We care a

| *E5 | E6 | E7 | riff 1 |
lot.   (We care a

all chords played over a constant E pedal

Verse 1

E5   E6
Lot) about disasters, fires, floods and killer bees

    E7   E6
A - bout the Nasa shuttle falling in the sea (We care a

E5   E6
Lot) about starvation and the food that Live Aid bought (We care a

E7   E6 | riff 1 x2 |
Lot) about disease, baby, Rock Hudson, rock yeah!

Chorus 1

| E5* | A5 D5 |
        Woah.

E5*   A5   D5 | E5* | A5 D5 |
It's a dirty job but someone's gotta do it.

    E5*   A5   D5
Oh it's a dirty job but someone's gotta do it. (We care a

| E5 | E6 | E7 | E6 |
Lot.   We care a

| E5 | E6 | E7 | riff 1(E6) |
Lot.(We care a   (We care a

Verse 2

E5   E6
Lot) about the gamblers and the pushers and the geeks (We care a

    E7   E6
Lot) about the smack and crack and wack that hits the streets (We care a

E5   **E6**
Lot) about the welfare of all you boys and girls (We care a
          E7   **E6** | **riff 1 x2** |
Lot) about you people 'cos we're out to save the world, yeah!

              E5*   **A5**   **D5**
Chorus 2   ‖: Oh it's a dirty job but someone's gotta do it,
          E5*   **A5**   **D5**
Oh it's a dirty job but someone's gotta do it,
          E5*   **A5**   **D5**
Said it's a dirty job but someone's gotta do it,
          E5*   **A5**   **D5**
Oh it's a dirty job but someone's gotta do it. :‖
                              (2° only) (We care a

                    N.C.
Verse 3   Lot) about the Army, Navy, Air Force and Marines, (We care a

Lot) about the NY, SF and LAPD (We care a

Lot) about you people, (We care a

Lot) about your guns, (We care a

Lot) about the wars we're fighting, gee that looks like fun. (We care a
E5   **E6**
Lot) about the Garbage Pail Kids, they never lie (We care a
E5   **E6**
Lot) about Transformers, 'cos there's more than meets the eyes (We care a
E5   **E6**
Lot) about the little things, the bigger days, we top (We care a
E7   **E6** | **riff 1 x2** |
Lot) about you people, yeah, you bet we care a lot.

          | **E5*** | **A5** **D5** | **E5*** | **A5** **D5** |
Chorus 3   Wooh.
          | **E5*** | **A5** **D5** | **E5*** | **A5** **D5** |

          | **E5*** | **A5** **D5** ‖
                    Wooh.
              E5*   **A5***   **D5**
          ‖: Said it's a dirty job but someone's gotta do it,
          E5*   **A5***   **D5**
Said it's a dirty job but someone's gotta do it... :‖ *Play 3 times*
                              (2° only) Wooh.
          E5*   **A5**   **D5**
And it's a dirty song but someone's gotta sing it.

          | **riff 1 x2** | **E5*** | ‖

THE FALL: Touch Sensitive

Words & Music by
Mark E. Smith, Julia Nagle & Steve Hitchcock

B   A5   E   A

fr7   fr5   × × × ×

Tune guitar slightly flat

Intro

| B   A5 | B   A5 | B   A5 | B   A5 ‖
Hey, hey, hey,

| E | A | E | A |
hey.

| E | A | E | A |
Hey, hey, hey,

| E | A ‖
hey.

E   A   E
I know, I know, I know. Hey! hey! hey!

      A   B
I know, I know, I know, I know.

      A   N.C.
I know, I know, I know, I know.

Verse 1

N.C.   B
In the cars or on the street,

N.C.   B
If you smile you are a creep.

N.C.   B
If you don't say it's very cold

N.C.   B   A5   B5
You are drunk and too old.

      A5   B   A5   B5
They say what a - bout the meek?

      A5   B   A5   B5
I say they've got a bloody cheek.

    A5   B   A5   B
Vanity and pre - sumption step out.

Chorus 1

B   E
Hey, hey, hey, hey.

      A   E   A
Living in the hard porn shop lately

      E   A   E   A
I say hey hey hey   Touch Sensi - tive

B   E
Hey, hey, hey, hey.

      A   E
I know, I know, I know, I know.

      A
I know, I know, I know.

```
        E              A
I know, I know, I know, I know.
        E              A
I know, I know, I know, I know.

        N.C.                    B
And you're dying for a pee,
        N.C.                    B
So you go behind a tree.
        N.C.                B
And a Star Wars police vehicle pulls up,
                    B    A5   B5
I say gimme a taxi.
                A5       B
Touch Sen - sitive.
                A5       B     A5      B     A5      B
Touch Sen - sitive.
```

Verse 2 (label appears to the left, aligned with "And you're dying for a pee")

```
| E          | E         | A        | E        | A         |        |
  Hey, hey, hey,  hey.
```

Bridge 1

```
(A)    E                        A
If you don't say it's very cold,
        E              A
You are drunk or too old.
                      E
It's Touch Sensitive.
A                    E
In the cars or on the street,
A                        E
If you smile you are a creep.
                A
I know, I know,   I know, I know. (It's touch sensitive.)
        E            A                E
I know, I know, I know. Hey, hey, hey, hey.
                    A                    E
If you don't say it's very cold (Hey, hey, hey, hey.)
        A              E
You are Touch Sensi - tive.
```

Verse 3

```
A                E    A                E
  Hey, hey, hey, hey,  Hey, hey, hey, hey.
A                E
Hey, hey, hey, hey.
            A              E
I know, I know, I know, I know.
            A              E
I know, I know, I know, I know.
            A              E
I know, I know.
```

Chorus 2

FUNKADELIC: Can You Get To That

Words & Music by
George Clinton & Eddie Harris

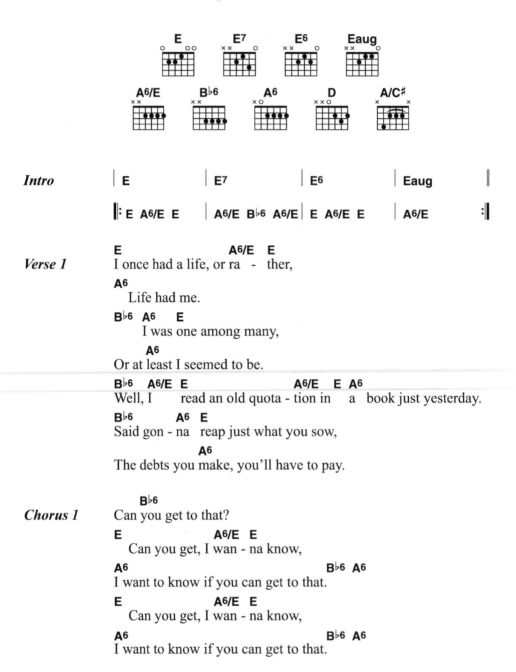

Intro | E | E7 | E6 | Eaug ‖

‖: E A6/E E | A6/E B♭6 A6/E | E A6/E E | A6/E :‖

Verse 1

E   A6/E E
I once had a life, or ra - ther,

A6
 Life had me.

B♭6 A6 E
 I was one among many,

   A6
Or at least I seemed to be.

B♭6 A6/E E   A6/E E A6
Well, I read an old quota - tion in a book just yesterday.

B♭6   A6 E
Said gon - na reap just what you sow,

    A6
The debts you make, you'll have to pay.

Chorus 1

   B♭6
Can you get to that?

E   A6/E E
 Can you get, I wan - na know,

A6   B♭6 A6
I want to know if you can get to that.

E   A6/E E
 Can you get, I wan - na know,

A6   B♭6 A6
I want to know if you can get to that.

<pre>
                          E   D   E
Verse 2   I recollect with a-mixed emo - tions,

                 All the good times we used to have.
                 D A/C♯   E
                    But you were making preparations,
                          D   E
                 For the coming separa - tion,

                 And you blew everything we had.

                 D A/C♯   (E)
Bridge 1   When you base your love on credit,

                 And your loving days are done.

                 Checks you signed with a-love and kisses,

                 Later come back signed insufficient funds.

                 Yeah, get to that!

                         E
Chorus 2   ‖: Get to that?
                                    A6/E E
                 Can you get, I wan - na know,
                 A6   B♭6 A6
                 I want to know if you can get to that.
                 E   A6/E E
                    Can you get, I wan - na know,
                 A6   B♭6 A6
                 I want to know if you can get to that.   :‖ *Play 3 times*

                         E
Bridge 2   When you base your life on credit,
                 D   E
                    And your loving days are done.
                 D   A/C♯ E
                 Checks you   signed with love and kisses,
                 D   E
                 Later come back signed insufficient funds.
                         D   A/C♯
                 Y'all get to that.

Chorus 3   ‖: As Chorus 1 :‖ *Repeat to fade*
</pre>

THE FLAMING LIPS:
The Yeah Yeah Yeah Song

Words & Music by
Wayne Coyne, Michael Ivins & Steven Droyd

E   C#m   A   F#m   G#m   F#7

Intro

‖: **N.C.**
Yeah, yeah, yeah, yeah,

Yeah, yeah, yeah, yeah,

Yeah, yeah, yeah, yeah,

Yeah, yeah, yeah. :‖ *Play 4 times*

| E E(G#bass) E | E E(G#bass) E | E C#m E |
N.C.
Yeah, yeah, yeah, yeah, yeah, yeah, yeah, yeah.

| E E(G#bass) E | C#m | E E(G#bass) E |
N.C.
Yeah, yeah, yeah, yeah, yeah, yeah, yeah, yeah.

Verse 1

              E
If you could blow up the world,

With the flick of a switch,

          A
Would you do it?
N.C.
Yeah, yeah, yeah, yeah, yeah, yeah, yeah, yeah.

          E
If you could make everybody poor,

Just so you could be rich,

     A
Would you do it?
N.C.
Yeah, yeah, yeah, yeah, yeah, yeah, yeah, yeah.

Verse 2

          E
If you could watch everybody work,

While you just lay on your back,

        A
Would you do it?

N.C.
Yeah, yeah, yeah, yeah, yeah, yeah, yeah, yeah.

         E
If you could take all the love,

Without giving any back,

        A
Would you do it?

N.C.
Yeah, yeah, yeah, yeah, yeah, yeah, yeah, yeah.

Pre chorus 1

          A   E
And so we cannot know our - selves,

    F#m   G#m
Or what we'd really do.

Chorus 1

   A   E   F#7
  With all your power, with all your power,

          A   E
With all your power, what would you do?

                      F#7
With all your power, with all your power,

          A   E
With all your power, what would you do?

Link

| E E(G#bass) E | E E(G#bass) E | E E(G#bass) E |

N.C.
No, no, no, no, no, no, no, no.

Verse 3

        E
If you could make your own money,

And then give it to everybody,

        A
Would you do it?

N.C.
No, no, no, no, no, no, no, no, no.

      E
If you knew all the answers,

And could give to the masses,

cont.

            A
Would you do it?
N.C.
No, no, no, no, no, no.

           E
Are you crazy?

     A
It's a very dangerous thing to do,
N.C.
Exactly what you want.

           A   **E**

Pre chorus 2 Because you cannot know your - self,

       F♯m   **G♯m**
Or what you'd really do.

      A   **E**   **F♯7**

Chorus 2   With all your power, with all your power,

         A   **E**
With all your power, what would you do?

             F♯7
With all your power, with all your power,

         A
With all your power, what would you,

      N.C.

Interlude Do, do, do, do, do, do, do, do,

Do, do, do, do, do, do, do, do,

Do, do, do, do, do, do, do, do,

Do, do, do, do, do, do, do.

$\|$: **N.C.**
  Yeah, yeah, yeah, yeah,

Yeah, yeah, yeah, yeah,

Yeah, yeah, yeah, yeah,

Yeah, yeah, yeah. :$\|$ *Play 8 times*

| (E) | (E) | (E) | (E) $\|$

        E   **F♯7**

Chorus 3 $\|$: With all your power, with all your power,

         A   **E**
With all your power, what would you do? :$\|$ *Play 3 times*

THE JIMI HENDRIX EXPERIENCE:
Purple Haze

Words & Music by
Jimi Hendrix

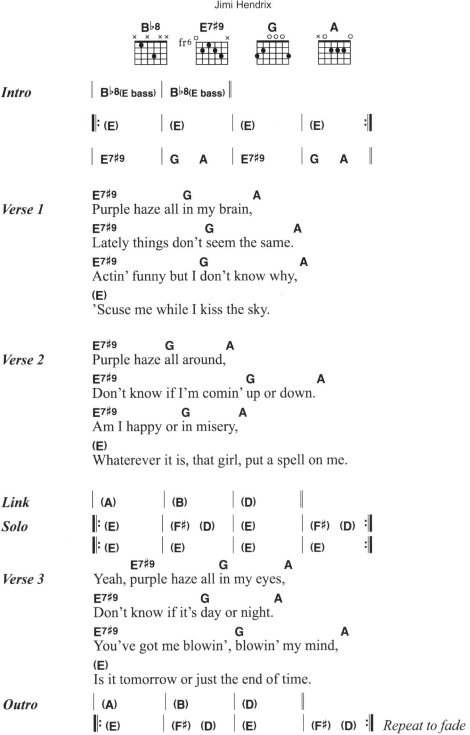

Intro

| B♭8(E bass) | B♭8(E bass) ‖

‖: (E) | (E) | (E) | (E) :‖

| E7♯9 | G A | E7♯9 | G A ‖

Verse 1

E7♯9   G   A
Purple haze all in my brain,
E7♯9   G   A
Lately things don't seem the same.
E7♯9   G   A
Actin' funny but I don't know why,
(E)
'Scuse me while I kiss the sky.

Verse 2

E7♯9   G   A
Purple haze all around,
E7♯9   G   A
Don't know if I'm comin' up or down.
E7♯9   G   A
Am I happy or in misery,
(E)
Whaterever it is, that girl, put a spell on me.

Link

| (A) | (B) | (D) ‖

Solo

‖: (E) | (F♯) (D) | (E) | (F♯) (D) :‖

‖: (E) | (E) | (E) | (E) :‖

Verse 3

             E7♯9   G   A
Yeah, purple haze all in my eyes,
E7♯9   G   A
Don't know if it's day or night.
E7♯9   G   A
You've got me blowin', blowin' my mind,
(E)
Is it tomorrow or just the end of time.

Outro

| (A) | (B) | (D) ‖

‖: (E) | (F♯) (D) | (E) | (F♯) (D) :‖ *Repeat to fade*

GANG OF FOUR: Damaged Goods

Words & Music by
Jonathan King, David Allen, Andrew Gill & Hugo Burnham

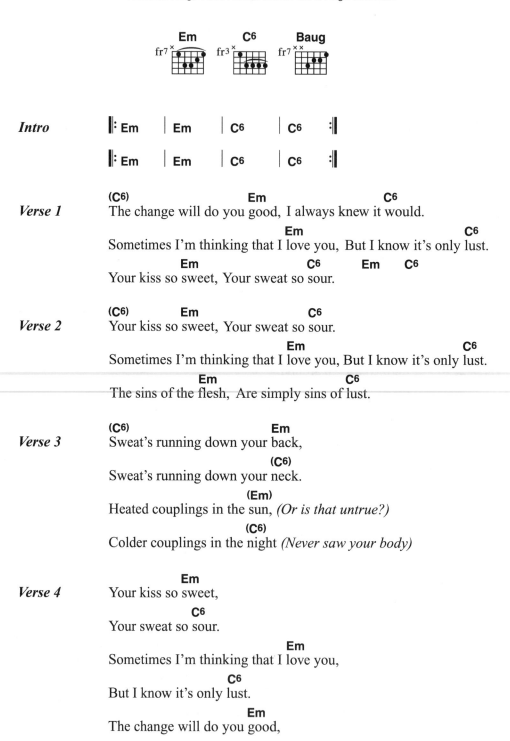

Intro

‖: Em | Em | C6 | C6 :‖

‖: Em | Em | C6 | C6 :‖

Verse 1

(C6)   Em   C6
The change will do you good, I always knew it would.

       Em   C6
Sometimes I'm thinking that I love you, But I know it's only lust.

       Em   C6   Em   C6
Your kiss so sweet, Your sweat so sour.

Verse 2

(C6)   Em   C6
Your kiss so sweet, Your sweat so sour.

       Em   C6
Sometimes I'm thinking that I love you, But I know it's only lust.

       Em   C6
The sins of the flesh, Are simply sins of lust.

Verse 3

(C6)   Em
Sweat's running down your back,

       (C6)
Sweat's running down your neck.

       (Em)
Heated couplings in the sun, *(Or is that untrue?)*

       (C6)
Colder couplings in the night *(Never saw your body)*

Verse 4

       Em
Your kiss so sweet,

       C6
Your sweat so sour.

       Em
Sometimes I'm thinking that I love you,

       C6
But I know it's only lust.

       Em
The change will do you good,

C6
I always knew it would.

                                 Em
You know the change will do you good.

                                 C6
You know the change will do you good.

Link | N.C. | N.C. | N.C. | N.C. ‖
Drums

                N.C.
Bridge Damaged goods, Send them back.
                I can't work, I can't achieve,
                Send me back. Open the till,
                Give me the change.
                You said would do me good.
                Refund the cost,   **(Em)**
                You said you're cheap but you're too much.

Verse 5   As Verse 4

        ‖: Em | Em | C6 | C6 :‖

        (C6)   **Em**
Outro   I'm kissing you good - bye.

        (Goodbye, goodbye, goodbye, goodbye, goodbye.)
                            C6
        I'm kissing you good - bye. (Goodbye, goodbye, goodbye.)
                            Em
        I'm kissing you good - bye

        (Goodbye, goodbye, goodbye, goodbye, goodbye.)
                            C6
        I'm kissing you good - bye (Goodbye, goodbye, goodbye.)
                            Em
        I'm kissing you good - bye

        (Goodbye, goodbye, goodbye, goodbye, goodbye.)
                            C6
        I'm kissing you good - bye (Goodbye, goodbye, goodbye.)
        Em
        Goodbye, goodbye, goodbye, goodbye, goodbye.
        C6
        Goodbye, goodbye, goodbye.
        Em
        Goodbye, goodbye, goodbye, goodbye, goodbye.
        C6
        Goodbye, goodbye, goodbye.

        | Em | Em | Baug ‖

GENE LOVES JEZEBEL: Desire

Words & Music by
Jay Aston

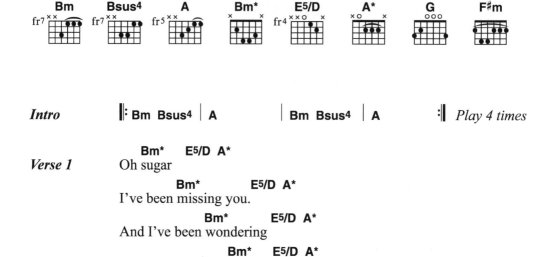

Intro   ‖: Bm Bsus4 | A | Bm Bsus4 | A   :‖   *Play 4 times*

Verse 1
       Bm*   **E5/D A***
Oh sugar

          Bm*   **E5/D A***
I've been missing you.

              Bm*   **E5/D A***
And I've been wondering

               Bm* **E5/D A***
Where it is you're hiding.

            Bm* **E5/D A* Bm***
I've been a ball of fire

         E5/D   **A* Bm***
In your arms de - sire.

           E5/D   **A***
And I've been wonder - ing

          Bm* **E5/D A***
Where it is you're hiding.

Chorus 1
Bm   **A**   **Bm**
  What you get is what you seek.

   A
Desire.

Bm   **A**   **Bm**
  What you get is what you seek.

   A
Desire.

Verse 2

Bm* E5/D A*
Oh honey,

Bm* E5/D A*
I won't be kissing you.

Bm* E5/D A*
And I've been wondering

Bm* E5/D A*
Where it is you're hiding.

Bm* E5/D A* Bm*
I've been a ball of fire

E5/D A* Bm*
In your arms de - sire.

E5/D A*
And I've been wonder - ing

Bm* E5/D A*
Where it is you're hiding.

Chorus 2

As Chorus 1

Chorus 3

As Chorus 1

Bridge

‖: Bm* | A* | G | F♯m :‖

Guitar solo

‖: Bm | A | Bm | A :‖

Verse 3

Bm* E5/D A* Bm* E5/D A*
I've had my ears to the ground, to the ground.

Bm* E5/D A* Bm* E5/D A*
I'm just trying to find out what you're hiding.

What is the mystery?

Chorus 4

Bm A Bm
‖: What you get is what you seek.

A
De - sire.

Bm A Bm
What you get is what you seek.

A
De - sire. :‖ *Play 4 times then fade out*

THE GUN CLUB: Sex Beat

Words & Music by
Jeffrey Pierce

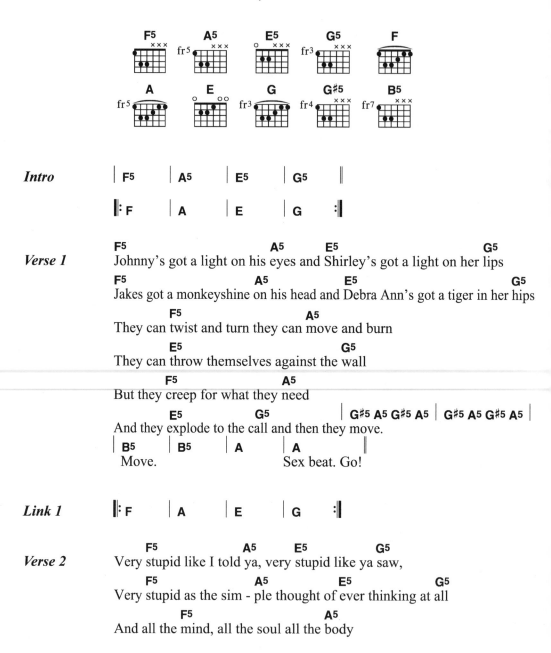

Intro | F5 | A5 | E5 | G5 ‖

‖: F | A | E | G :‖

Verse 1
F5   A5   E5   G5
Johnny's got a light on his eyes and Shirley's got a light on her lips
F5   A5   E5   G5
Jakes got a monkeyshine on his head and Debra Ann's got a tiger in her hips
           F5   A5
They can twist and turn they can move and burn
           E5   G5
They can throw themselves against the wall
           F5   A5
But they creep for what they need
           E5   G5 | G#5 A5 G#5 A5 | G#5 A5 G#5 A5 |
And they explode to the call and then they move.
| B5 | B5 | A | A ‖
   Move.   Sex beat. Go!

Link 1 ‖: F | A | E | G :‖

Verse 2
           F5   A5   E5   G5
Very stupid like I told ya, very stupid like ya saw,
           F5   A5   E5   G5
Very stupid as the sim - ple thought of ever thinking at all
                   F5   A5
And all the mind, all the soul all the body

cont.

           E5   **G5**
All we know all the things that should have made us whole

     F5   **A5**   **E5**   **G5**
All the colourless security was only so we could go and

| **G♯5 A5 G♯5 A5** | **G♯5 A5 G♯5 A5** |
move.

| **B5** | **B5** | **A** | **A** ‖
 Move.   Sex beat. Drop!

Link 2 ‖: **F** | **A** | **E** | **G** :‖

     F5   **A5**   **E5**   **G5**
Verse 3 And yes you do look cool and by the floodlights so blue,

     F5   **A5**   **E5**   **G5**
You make my tropi - cal apartment bed, your sacrificial pool.

     F5   **A5**   **E5**   **G5**
My body in the water and my heart is in your hand,

     F5   **A5**   **E5**   **G5**
So this is the way you choose to send me to the judgement land.

       | **G♯5 A5 G♯5 A5** | **G♯5 A5 G♯5 A5** |
So you can't move.

| **B5** | **B5** | **A** | **A** ‖
 Move.   Sex beat. Go!

Link 3 ‖: **F** | **A** | **E** | **G** :‖

     F5   **A5**   **E5**   **G5**
Verse 4 And every day at three you throw me down by the Christmas tree,

    F5   **A5**   **E5**   **G5**
I watched your lights blink on and off while you start your fun with me.

     F5   **A5**   **E5**   **G5**
I, I know your reasons and I, I know your goals,

    F5   **A5**   **E5**   **G5**
We can fuck forever but you will never get my soul.

      | **G♯5 A5 G♯5 A5** | **G♯5 A5 G♯5 A5** |
So you can move.   So you can move.

      B5
So you can move

         A
So you can move so you can

Sex beat.

THE HAPPY MONDAYS: Kinky Afro

Words & Music by
Shaun Ryder, Paul Ryder, Mark Day & Paul Davis

G/A   Em/A   Em⁷   A⁷

Capo third fret

Intro

| G/A | Em/A | G/A | Em/A ||

||: Em⁷ | A⁷ | Em⁷ | A⁷ :||

Verse 1

Em⁷   A⁷
Son, I'm 30
    Em⁷   A⁷
I only went with your mother 'cause she's dirty
    Em⁷   A⁷
And I don't   have a decent bone in me
     Em⁷   A⁷
What you get is just what you see yeah
    Em⁷   A⁷
I see it so I take it freely
      Em⁷   A⁷
And all the bad piss ugly things I feed me
    Em⁷   A⁷
I never help or give to the needy
     Em⁷   A⁷
Come on and see me

Chorus 1

Em⁷   A⁷
Yippee-ippee-ey-ey-ay-yey-yey
    Em⁷   A⁷
I had to crucify some brother to - day
      Em⁷
And I don't   dig what you gotta say
       Em⁷   A⁷
So come on and say it
     Em⁷   A⁷
Come on and tell me twice

Link 1

||: Em⁷ | A⁷ :||

Verse 2

       Em7   **A7**
I said dad you're shabby,

            Em7   **A7**
You run a - round and groove like a baggy,

            Em7   **A7**
You're only here just out of habit,

              Em7   **A7**
All that's mine you might as well have it.

             Em7   **A7**
You take ten feet back and then stab it,

                 Em7 **A7**
Spray it on and tag   it.

      Em7
So sack on me,

   A7
I can't stand the needy.

Em7   **A7**
Get around here if you're asking you're feeling.

Chorus 2   As Chorus 1

Link 2   ‖: **Em7** | **A7**   :‖ *Play 7 times*

            Em7
So sack all the needy

          A7
I can't stand to leave it

            Em7   **A7**
You come around here and you put both your feet in

Chorus 3   **Em7**   **A7**
Yippee-ippee-ey-ey-ay-yey-yey

             Em7   **A7**
I had to crucify somebody to - day

                Em7   **A7**
And I don't   hear what you gotta say

                Em7 **A7**
So go on and say it

Chorus 4   As Chorus 1

Outro   ‖: **Em7** | **A7**   :‖ *Repeat to fade*

PJ HARVEY: The Letter

Words & Music by
Polly Jean Harvey

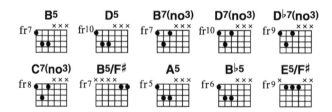

Verse 1

B5 D5   B5 D5
    Put the pen   to the paper.

B5 D5   B5 D5
    Press the envelope   with my scent.

B5 D5   B5 D5
    Can you see   in my handwriting,

B5 D5   B5 D5
    The curve of my 'G',   the longing?

Chorus 1

B7(no3)   D7(no3)
    Oh!

B7(no3)   D7(no3)
    Oh!

B7(no3)   D7(no3)
    Oh!

B7(no3)   D7(no3)   Db7(no3) C7(no3)
    Oh!

Verse 2

B5 D5   B5   D5
    Who is left   that writes these days?

B5 D5   B5 D5
    But you and me,   we'll be different.

B5 D5   B5 D5
    Take the cap   off your pen,

B5 D5   B5 D5
    And wet the envelope,   lick and lick it.

Chorus 2

B7(no3)   D7(no3)
           Oh!

B7(no3)   D7(no3)
           Oh!

B7(no3)   D7(no3)
           Oh!

B7(no3)   D7(no3) D♭7(no3) C7(no3)
           Oh!

Bridge

B5/F♯   A5 B♭5 B5
      I   need you

B5/F♯   A5   B♭5   B5
    The time is running   out

B5/F♯   A5 B♭5 B5
     Oh ba - by

B5/F♯ A5   B♭5 B5
     Can you hear me call?

Link

| B5 | D5 | B5 | D5 |

Verse 3

B5 D5   B5 D5
     It turns me on   to imagine

B5 D5   B5 D5
    Your blue eyes   on my words.

B5 D5   B5 D5
    Your beautiful pen,   take the cap off.

B5 D5   B5 D5
    Give me a sign,   and I'll come running.

Chorus 3

B7(no3)   D7(no3)
           Oh!

B7(no3)   D7(no3)
           Oh!

B7(no3)   D7(no3)
           Oh!

B7(no3)   D7(no3) D♭7(no3) C7(no3)
           Oh!

B7(no3)   D7(no3)   E5/F♯
           You!

B7(no3)   D7(no3)   E5/F♯   B7(no3)
           You,   it's you!

D7(no3)   E5/F♯
I   want you.

B7(no3)   D7(no3) D♭7(no3) C7(no3)   B5
           Oh,   it's   you!

HÜSKER DÜ: Makes No Sense At All

Words & Music by
Bob Mould

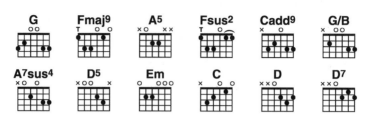

Verse 1

        G   **Fmaj9**   **A5**   **Fsus2**
Walking around with your head in the clouds,

Cadd9 **G/B**   **A7sus4 G D5**
Makes no sense at all.

G   **Fmaj9**   **A5**   **Fsus2**
Sell yourself short, but you're walking so tall,

  Cadd9 **G/B**   **A7sus4 G D5**
It makes no sense at all.

G   **Fmaj9**   **A5**   **Fsus2**
Is it impor - tant, you're yelling so loud,

Cadd9 **G/B**   **A7sus4 G D5**
Makes no sense at all.

G   **Fmaj9**   **A5**   **Fsus2**
Walking around with your head in the clouds,

Cadd9 **G/B**   **A7sus4 G**
Makes no sense at all.

Chorus 1

D5   **Cadd9 G/B** **A7sus4 G**
Makes no differ - ence at all,

D5   **Cadd9**   **G/B**   **A7sus4 G**
  Yeah, it makes no sense at all.

D5   **Cadd9 G/B** **A7sus4 G D5**
Makes no differ - ence at all,

Bridge 1

Em   **G**   **C**
  Well, I don't know why you want to tell me,

       Em   **D**
When I'm right or when I'm wrong.

     Em   **G**
It's the same thing in your mind,

       C   **Em**   **D**
The only time I'm right is when I play a - long,

           D7
When I play a - long.

Verse 2

G   Fmaj9 A5   Fsus2
Walking around with your head in the clouds,

Cadd9 G/B A7sus4 G D5
Makes no sense at all.

G   Fmaj9 A5   Fsus2
Sell yourself short, but you're walking so tall,

Cadd9 G/B A7sus4 G D5
Makes no sense at all.

G   Fmaj9 A5   Fsus2
Is it impor - tant, you're yelling so loud,

 Cadd9 G/B A7sus4 G D5
It makes no sense at all.

G   Fmaj9 A5   Fsus2
Walking around with your head in the clouds,

Cadd9 G/B A7sus4 G
Makes no sense at all.

Chorus 2

D5   Cadd9 G/B A7sus4 G
Makes no differ - ence at all,

D5   Cadd9 G/B A7sus4 G
 Yeah, it makes no sense at all.

D5   Cadd9 G/B A7sus4 G D5
Makes no differ - ence at all,

Bridge 2

Em   G   C
 Well, you con - cern yourself with evidence,

Em   D
It's evident to me.

    Em   G   C
Well, you say you've got the tiger by the tail,

    Em   D
But I don't see these things that way.

      D7
See these things that way.

Verse 3   As Verse 1

Chorus 3   As Chorus 1

Outro

G   Fmaj9 A5   Fsus2
Walking around with your head in the clouds,

 Cadd9 G/B A7sus4 G
It makes no sense at all.

INTERPOL: Obstacle 1

Words & Music by
Carlos Dengler, Daniel Kessler, Samuel Fogarino & Paul Banks

Intro

| F5 | F | A8 | Am | F5 | F | A8 | Am |
| F5 | | Am | | F5 | | Am | |
| F | | A8 | Am | F | | A8 | Am ‖

Verse 1

F5   Am   F5   Am
I wish I could eat the salt off of your last faded lips.

        F
We can cap the old times,

A8   Am F   A8
  Make playing only logical harm.

Am   F5
  We can cap the old lines,

Am   F5   Am
  Make playing that nothing else will change.

        F   A8   Am
But she can read, she can read, she can read, she can read, she's bad,

F   A8   Am
  She can read, she can read, she can read, she's bad, oh she's bad.

Link 1

| F* | F* | Am* | Am* | ‖

Chorus 1

      Fmaj7   C/E
But it's different now that I'm poor and aging,

    Am**   C
I'll never see his face again.

       Fmaj7   C/E   Am** C
You'll go stabbing yourself in   the neck.

Link 2

| F5 | F | A8 | Am | F5 | F | A8 | Am |

Verse 2

    Am   **F5**   **Am**
And we can find new ways of living,

F5   **Am**
Make playing only logical harm.

             F
And we can top the old times,

A8   **Am**   **F**   **A8**
   Play mak - ing that nothing else will change.

Am   **F5**   **Am**
But she can read, she can read, she can read, she can read, she's bad,

F5   **Am**   **F**
   She can read, she can read, she can read, she's bad,   oh, she's bad.

Link 3 | **F*** | **F*** | **Am*** | **Am***   ‖

Chorus 2   As Chorus 1 (x2)

Bridge

Am*
It's in the way that she poses.

        Am/C   **Am***
It's in the things that she puts in my hair.

        Am/C
Her stories are boring and stuff.

        Am*
She's always calling my bluff.

        Fmaj7
She puts the, she puts the weights into my little heart,

        D7sus2
And she gets in my room and she takes it apart.

Fmaj7
She puts the weights into my little heart,

      D7sus2   **Am/C**
I said she puts the weight into my little heart.

Interlude

   C   **Am****   **C**
   She puts the weight, she puts the weight,

        Am**   **Fmaj7**
She puts the weight, she puts the weight,

        D7sus2   **Fmaj7**
She puts the weight, she puts the weight,

        D7sus2
She puts the weight.

Outro

        Fmaj7
It's in the way that she walks,

        D7sus2
Her heaven is never enough.

        Fmaj7
She puts the weights in my heart,

        D7sus2   **Am/C**   **Am/B♭** **Am/C**
She puts the, she puts the weights into my little heart.

IGGY & THE STOOGES: Raw Power

Words & Music by
James Osterberg & James Williamson

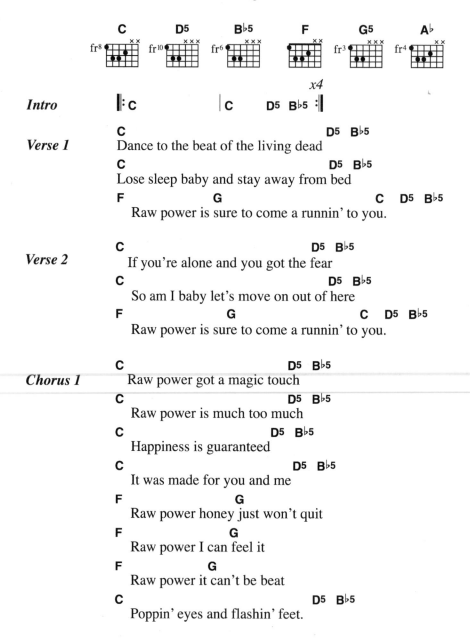

Intro

‖: C | C D5 B♭5 :‖ x4

Verse 1

C   D5 B♭5
Dance to the beat of the living dead
C   D5 B♭5
Lose sleep baby and stay away from bed
F   G   C D5 B♭5
 Raw power is sure to come a runnin' to you.

Verse 2

C   D5 B♭5
 If you're alone and you got the fear
C   D5 B♭5
 So am I baby let's move on out of here
F   G   C D5 B♭5
Raw power is sure to come a runnin' to you.

Chorus 1

C   D5 B♭5
Raw power got a magic touch
C   D5 B♭5
 Raw power is much too much
C   D5 B♭5
 Happiness is guaranteed
C   D5 B♭5
 It was made for you and me
F   G
 Raw power honey just won't quit
F   G
 Raw power I can feel it
F   G
 Raw power it can't be beat
C   D5 B♭5
 Poppin' eyes and flashin' feet.

Bridge

A♭
  Don't you try

                                    C   **D5** **B♭5**
Don't you try to tell me what to do

A♭   **C** **D5** **B♭5**
  Everybody's always tryin' to tell me what to do.

| **C** | | **C**   **D5** **B♭5** |

Verse 3

C   **D5** **B♭5**
I look in the eyes of the savage girl

C   **D5** **B♭5**
Fall deep in love in the underworld

F   **G**   **C** **D5** **B♭5**
  Raw power is sure to come a runnin' to you.

Verse 4

C   **D5** **B♭5**
  If you're alone and you got the shakes

C   **D5**   **B♭5**
  So am I baby and I got what it takes

F   **G**   **C** **D5** **B♭5**
  Raw power is sure to come a runnin' to you.

Chorus 2

C   **D5** **B♭5**
  Raw power got a healin' hand

C   **D5** **B♭5**
  Raw power can destroy a man

C   **D5** **B♭5**
  Raw power is more than soul

C   **D5** **B♭5**
  Has got a son called rock and roll

F   **G**
  Raw power honey just won't quit

F   **G**
  Raw power I can feel it

F   **G**
  Raw power honey can't be beat

C   **D5** **B♭5**
  Get down baby and kiss my feet.

Bridge 2

Aᵇ   C   D5 Bᵇ5

Aᵇ		**C**	**D5** **Bᵇ5**

Everybody's always tryin' to tell me what to do

Aᵇ — Don't you try, don't you try to tell me what to do — **C** **D5** **Bᵇ5**

Aᵇ — Everybody's always tryin' to tell me what to do — **C** **D5** **Bᵇ5**

Aᵇ — Don't you try, don't you try to tell me what to do. — **C** **D5** **Bᵇ5**

Chorus 3

Aᵇ — Raw power's got no place to go — **C** **D5** **Bᵇ5**

Aᵇ — Raw power honey, it don't want to know — **C** **D5** **Bᵇ5**

Aᵇ — Raw power is a guaranteed O.D. — **C** **D5** **Bᵇ5**

Aᵇ — Raw power is laughin' at you and me. — **C** **D5** **Bᵇ5**

(And this is what I wanta know)

Outro

Aᵇ   **C**   **D5**
Can you feel it? Can you feel it?

Bᵇ5   **Aᵇ**   **C**   **D5**
Oh honey, feel it! Can you feel it?

Bᵇ5   **Aᵇ**   **C**   **D5**
Can you feel it? Can you feel it?

Bᵇ5   **Aᵇ**   **C**   **D5**
Raw power! Raw power!

Bᵇ5   **Aᵇ**   **C**   **D5**
Raw power! Raw power!

Bᵇ5   **Aᵇ**   **C**   **D5**
Can you feel it? Feel it!

Bᵇ5   **Aᵇ**   **C**   **D5**
Raw power! Raw power!

Bᵇ5   **Aᵇ**   **C**   **D5**
Raw power! Raw power!

Bᵇ5   **Aᵇ**   **C**   **D5**
Raw power! Raw power!

Bᵇ5   **C**   **D5** **Bᵇ5**
Can you feel it, baby?

‖: **Aᵇ** | **Aᵇ** | **C** | **C**   **D5** **Bᵇ5** :‖   *Repeat to fade*

JOY DIVISION: Atmosphere

Words & Music by
Peter Hook, Bernard Sumner, Stephen Morris & Ian Curtis

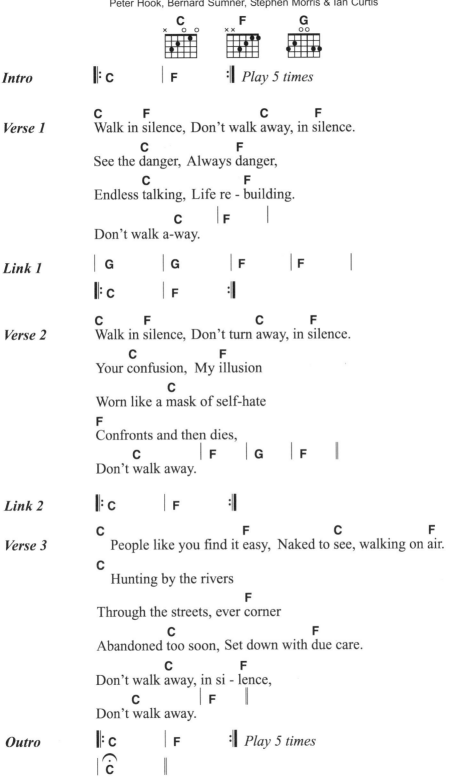

Intro   ‖: C | F :‖ *Play 5 times*

Verse 1
C   F   C   F
Walk in silence, Don't walk away, in silence.
         C   F
See the danger, Always danger,
         C   F
Endless talking, Life re - building.
                 C | F |
Don't walk a-way.

Link 1 | G | G | F | F |
‖: C | F   :‖

Verse 2
C   F   C   F
Walk in silence, Don't turn away, in silence.
         C   F
Your confusion, My illusion
              C
Worn like a mask of self-hate
F
Confronts and then dies,
         C | F | G | F   ‖
Don't walk away.

Link 2   ‖: C | F   :‖

Verse 3
C   F   C   F
    People like you find it easy, Naked to see, walking on air.
C
    Hunting by the rivers
                         F
Through the streets, ever corner
              C   F
Abandoned too soon, Set down with due care.
         C   F
Don't walk away, in si - lence,
         C | F   ‖
Don't walk away.

Outro   ‖: C | F   :‖ *Play 5 times*
| C   ‖

JANE'S ADDICTION: Been Caught Stealing

Words & Music by
Perry Farrell, David Navarro, Stephen Perkins & Eric Avery

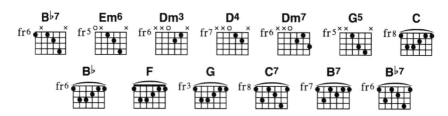

Intro | B♭7 Em6 | Dm3/(Gbass) | D4/(G) | Dm3/(G) |

| D4/(G) | Dm3/(G) | D4/(G) | Dm7/(G) | G5 ‖

Verse 1

        Dm3/(G)   **D4/(G)**
I've been caught stealing; once when I was five——

   Dm3/(G)
I enjoy steal - ing.

         D4/(G)
It's just as simple as that.

      Dm3/(G)   **D4/(G)**
Well, it's just a   simple fact.

         Dm3
When I want some - thing, man, I

      D4
Don't want to pay for it.

 C   **N.C.**   **C**
I walk right through the door.

B♭ **C** **B♭**   **F** **G**
Walk right through the door.

C   **C7**
  Hey all right! If I get by,

B♭7 **Em6** **N.C.** **Dm3/(G)**   **D4/(G)**
    It's mine. Mine all mine! Hey!

Link 1 | Dm3/(G) | D4/(G) | Dm3/(G) |

Verse 2

D4/(G)   **Dm3/(G)**
  Yeah my girl, she's one too.

         D4/(G)
She'll go and get her a skirt.

       Dm3/(G)
Stick it under her shirt.

<pre>
                          D4/(G)
She grabbed a razor for me.
              Dm3/(G)   D4/(G)
And she   did it just like that.
                  Dm3/(G)   D4/(G)
When she wants something man, she don't want to pay for it.
        C   N.C.   C
She walk right through the door.
B♭   C   B♭   F   G
Walk right through the door.
C   C7
   Hey all right!   If I get by,
B♭7 Em6 N.C. Dm3/(G)   D4/(G)
             It's mine. Mine all mine! Let's go!
</pre>

Guitar solo   ‖: Dm3/(G) | D4/(G) :‖ *Play 4 times*

Bridge
<pre>
       C   B♭ B7 B♭7 B7
Da da da da da da da da da da da da da da da da,
       C   B♭ B7 B♭7 B7
Da da da da da da da da da da da da da da da da
</pre>

Bass link | (G) | (G) | (G) | (G)   ‖

Verse 3
<pre>
             Dm3/(G)
We sat around the pile.
           D4/(G)
We sat and laughed.
           Dm3/(G)
We sat and laughed and
                   D4/(G)
Waved it into the air!
           Dm3/(G) N.C.   D4/(G)
And we   did it just like that.
                      Dm3/(G)   D4/(G)
When we wants some - thing man, we don't want to pay for it.
        C   N.C.   C
We walk right through the door.
B♭   C   B♭   F   G
Walk right through the door.
C   C7   B♭7   Em6
   Hey all right!   If I get by,
</pre>

Outro
<pre>
N.C. C
It's mine, mine, mine, mine,
C7
Mine, mine, mine... mine, mine, all mine...
B♭7 Em6   G
             It's mine.
</pre>

THE JESUS AND MARY CHAIN: April Skies

Words & Music by
James Reid & William Reid

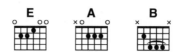

Tune guitar down a semitone

Intro | E | E   ‖

Verse 1
    E   A
Hey honey what you trying to say,

                                  B
As I stand here, don't you walk away,

    A   B   E
And the world comes tumbling down.

                    A
Hand in hand in a violent life,

                          B
Making love on the edge of a knife,

    A   B   E
And the world comes tumbling down.

Bridge
           A
And it's hard for me to say,

           E
And it's hard for me to stay.

       A
I'm going down to be by myself,

       E
I'm going back for the good of my health.

        B
And there's one thing I couldn't do,

      A
Sacri - fice myself to you,

       (E)
Sacri - fice.

Interlude | E | E | A | A |
             (- fice.)
            | E | E | A | A |

            | B | B | A | A   ‖

Verse 2

       E   A
Baby, baby I just can't see
                  E
Just what you mean to me.
                         A
I take my aim and I fake my words,
                B
I'm just your long time curse.
               A
And if you walk away I can't take it.
             E
But that's the way that you are,
             A
And that's the things that you say.
           E
But now you've gone too far,
        A
With all the things you say.
B
Get back to where you come from
   A
I can't help it

Chorus

Under the April skies,

Under the April skies,

Under the April sun,

Under the April skies.

Ooh.————

Ooh.————

Ooh.————

Ooh.————

Under the April sun,

Under the April sun,

Under the April skies.

Under the April sun,

Under the April skies.

KILLING JOKE: Love Like Blood

Words & Music by
Jaz Coleman, Kevin Walker, Paul Raven & Paul Ferguson

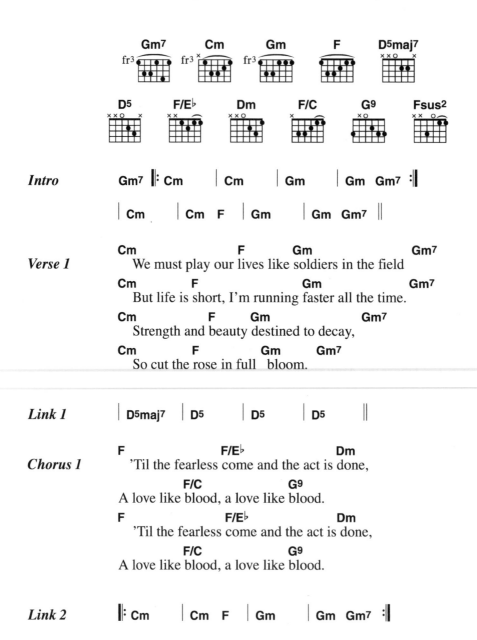

Intro

Gm7 ‖: Cm | Cm | Gm | Gm Gm7 :‖

| Cm | Cm F | Gm | Gm Gm7 ‖

Verse 1

Cm   F   Gm   Gm7
We must play our lives like soldiers in the field

Cm   F   Gm   Gm7
But life is short, I'm running faster all the time.

Cm   F   Gm   Gm7
Strength and beauty destined to decay,

Cm   F   Gm   Gm7
So cut the rose in full   bloom.

Link 1

| D5maj7 | D5 | D5 | D5 ‖

Chorus 1

F   F/E♭   Dm
'Til the fearless come and the act is done,

         F/C   G9
A love like blood, a love like blood.

F   F/E♭   Dm
'Til the fearless come and the act is done,

         F/C   G9
A love like blood, a love like blood.

Link 2

‖: Cm | Cm F | Gm | Gm Gm7 :‖

Verse 2

Cm   F   Gm   Gm⁷
Everyday, through all frustration and despair,

Cm   F   Gm   Gm⁷
Love and hate fight with burning hearts

Cm   F   Gm   Gm⁷
'Til legends live and each man is god again

Cm   F   Gm   Gm⁷
And self-preservation rules the day no more.

Verse 3

Cm   F   Gm   Gm⁷
We must dream of promised lands and fields

Cm   F   Gm   Gm⁷
That never fade in season.

Cm   F   Gm   Gm⁷
As we move towards no end we learn to die.

Cm   F   Gm   Gm⁷
Red tears are shed on grey.

Link 3 | D5maj⁷ | D5 | D5 | D5 ||

Chorus 2

F   F/E♭   Dm
'Til the fearless come and the act is done,

            F/C   G⁹
A love like blood, a love like blood.

F   F/E♭   Dm
'Til the fearless come and the act is done,

            F/C   G⁹
A love like blood, a love like blood.

Instrumental ||: D5 | D5 D5maj⁷ | D5 | D5 Fsus2 :||

                 | D5 D5maj⁷ | D5 Fsus2 | D5 D5maj⁷ | D5 Fsus2 ||

Chorus 3

F   F/E♭   Dm
'Til the fearless come and the act is done,

            F/C   G⁹
A love like blood, a love like blood.

F   F/E♭   Dm
'Til the fearless come and the act is done,

            F/C
A love like blood.
          Fade out

KRAFTWERK: The Model

Words & Music by
Ralf Hutter, Karl Bartos & Emil Schult

Am   Em   C   Bm   G   E

Intro   ‖: Am | Em | Am | Em :‖

Verse 1
Am   Em   Am Em
She's a model and she's looking good
      Am   Em   Am Em
I'd like to take her home that's understood
        Am   Em   Am Em
She plays hard to get she smiles from time to time
        Am   Em   Am Em
It only takes a camera to change her mind

Link 1 | C | Bm | G | G |
              | C | Bm | E | E ‖

Verse 2
           Am   Em   Am Em
She's going out tonight but drinking just champagne
        Am   Em   Am Em
And she has been checking nearly all the men
          Am   Em   Am Em
She's playing her game and you can hear them say
Am   Em   Am Em
She is looking good, for beauty we will pay

Link 2   As Link 1

Instr. 1   ‖: Am | Em | Am | Em :‖ *Play 4 times*

Link 3   As Link 1

Verse 3
           Am   Em   Am Em
She's posing for consumer products now and then
         Am   Em   Am Em
For every camera she gives the best she can
       Am   Em   Am Em
I saw her on the cover of a magazine
           Am   Em   Am Em
Now she's a big success, I want to meet her again

Instr. 2   ‖: Am | Em | Am | Em :‖ *Play 3 times*
                | Am | Em | Am | (Am) ‖
                        let ring...

LOW: Like A Forest

Words & Music by
Mimi Parker, Zak Sally & George Sparhawk

Asus⁴   **A**   **F♯m**   **F**   **E**   **D**   **Dm**   **E⁷**

Tune guitar down a semitone

Intro

| Asus⁴ A Asus⁴ A | Asus⁴ A Asus⁴ A |

| Asus⁴ A Asus⁴ A | Asus⁴ A Asus⁴ A |

| A | A | A | A |

Verse 1

A   F♯m
Black, like a forest and still like a lion,

F
My knees are bended,

E
We used to speak a different language.

A   F♯m
I wasted my breath on words soon forgotten,

F
Left unattended,

          E
They're moving their feet, but nobody's dancing.

Chorus 1

D Dm   F♯m
Ah,   take your time.

D   E   E⁷
Ah, take your time._____

Verse 2

A   F♯m
How can I blame you for all of the screaming

    F
That I've had to turn to?

E   A   F♯m F E A
Just in time to go off in my hands._____

THE LIBERTINES: Last Post On The Bugle

Words & Music by
Pete Doherty, Carl Barat & Michael Bower

Cm   F   B♭   Gm   D   G   E♭

Intro | (Gm) | (Gm) | (Gm) | (Gm) ‖

‖: Cm | F | B♭ | Gm :‖

| E♭ | Gm | E♭ ‖

Chorus 1
Gm   F   B♭   D   Gm
  If I have to go,   I will be thinking of your love.
                   F   B♭
Oh, somehow you'll know, You will know,
D
Thinking of your love.

Verse 1
Cm   F
Slyly they whispered a - way,
            B♭
As I played the Last Post on the bugle,
Gm
I heard them say,
       Cm   F
Oh, "That boy's no different to - day."
      Gm
Except in every single way.

Chorus 2
Gm   F   B♭   D   Gm
  If I have to go,   I will be thinking of your love.
                F   B♭
Oh, somehow you'll know, You'll just know,
D
Thinking of your love.

Verse 2
Cm   F
Oh, I was carried a - way,
        B♭
Caught up in an affray,
     Gm
As they led him away, he sang.
Cm   F
We'll meet again some - day,
     Gm
Oh, my boy, there's a price to pay.

Chorus 3

Gm   F B♭   D   Gm
If I have to go,   I will be thinking of your love.

                    F   B♭
Oh, somehow you'll know, I don't know how, but you'll know.

D
Thinking of your love.

Solo

‖: (Gm) | B♭ | F | Gm :‖

| E♭ | Gm | E♭ | (Gm) | (Gm) ‖

Bridge

Inside I felt so, so alone,

Cm
   Locked in a room,

F   B♭
   Waiting for kingdom come,

                 Gm
Although I felt e - lated,

I felt like I was scum.

Verse 4

Cm   F
I was carried a - way,

          B♭
Caught up in an affray,

          Gm
As they led him away, he sang.

Cm   F
We'll meet again some - day,

          Gm
Oh, my boy, there's a price to pay.

              Cm   F
Feels like I've never been a - way,

                  B♭   Gm
Though it's been longer than I could possibly say.

Cm   F
I've been wandering the market,

          B♭   Gm   Cm   F
Carrying a sign, saying the end of the world is nigh,

        B♭   Gm
I'm glad to see we're still tight.

        Cm   F
The bonds that tie a man are tight,

B♭   G
Yet we do what we do,

Outro

E♭   Gm
With ritual habitua - lity,

E♭   G
All through the night.

THE LONG RYDERS:
Looking For Lewis And Clark

Words & Music by
Sid Griffin

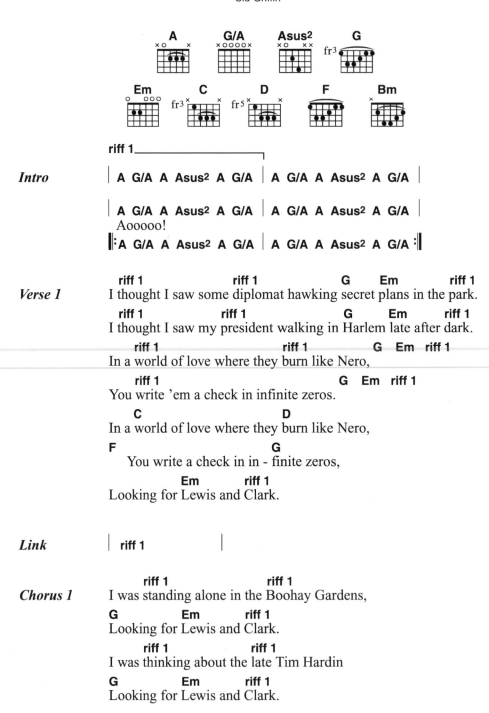

riff 1

Intro

| A G/A A Asus2 A G/A | A G/A A Asus2 A G/A |

| A G/A A Asus2 A G/A | A G/A A Asus2 A G/A |
 Aooooo!
‖: A G/A A Asus2 A G/A | A G/A A Asus2 A G/A :‖

Verse 1

     riff 1   **riff 1**   **G**   **Em**   **riff 1**
I thought I saw some diplomat hawking secret plans in the park.

     riff 1   **riff 1**   **G**   **Em**   **riff 1**
I thought I saw my president walking in Harlem late after dark.

       riff 1   **riff 1**   **G** **Em** **riff 1**
In a world of love where they burn like Nero,

      riff 1   **G** **Em** **riff 1**
You write 'em a check in infinite zeros.

      C   **D**
In a world of love where they burn like Nero,

F   **G**
    You write a check in in - finite zeros,

            Em   **riff 1**
Looking for Lewis and Clark.

Link

| **riff 1** |

Chorus 1

      riff 1   **riff 1**
I was standing alone in the Boohay Gardens,

G   **Em**   **riff 1**
Looking for Lewis and Clark.

      riff 1   **riff 1**
I was thinking about the late Tim Hardin

G   **Em**   **riff 1**
Looking for Lewis and Clark.

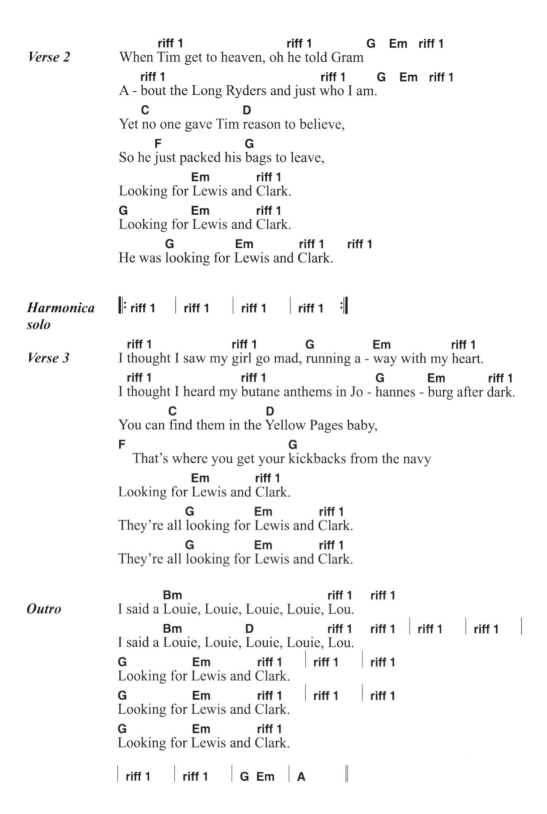

Verse 2

    riff 1   **riff 1**   **G** **Em** **riff 1**
When Tim get to heaven, oh he told Gram

    riff 1   **riff 1**   **G** **Em** **riff 1**
A - bout the Long Ryders and just who I am.

   C   **D**
Yet no one gave Tim reason to believe,

     F   **G**
So he just packed his bags to leave,

       Em   **riff 1**
Looking for Lewis and Clark.

G   **Em**   **riff 1**
Looking for Lewis and Clark.

     G   **Em**   **riff 1**   **riff 1**
He was looking for Lewis and Clark.

Harmonica solo   ‖: **riff 1** | **riff 1** | **riff 1** | **riff 1** :‖

Verse 3

   riff 1   **riff 1**   **G**   **Em**   **riff 1**
I thought I saw my girl go mad, running a - way with my heart.

   riff 1   **riff 1**   **G**   **Em**   **riff 1**
I thought I heard my butane anthems in Jo - hannes - burg after dark.

        C   **D**
You can find them in the Yellow Pages baby,

F   **G**
   That's where you get your kickbacks from the navy

       Em   **riff 1**
Looking for Lewis and Clark.

      G   **Em**   **riff 1**
They're all looking for Lewis and Clark.

      G   **Em**   **riff 1**
They're all looking for Lewis and Clark.

Outro

     Bm   **riff 1** **riff 1**
I said a Louie, Louie, Louie, Louie, Lou.

     Bm   **D**   **riff 1** **riff 1** | **riff 1** | **riff 1** |
I said a Louie, Louie, Louie, Louie, Lou.

G   **Em**   **riff 1** | **riff 1** | **riff 1**
Looking for Lewis and Clark.

G   **Em**   **riff 1** | **riff 1** | **riff 1**
Looking for Lewis and Clark.

G   **Em**   **riff 1**
Looking for Lewis and Clark.

| **riff 1** | **riff 1** | **G** **Em** | **A** ‖

LOVE: 7 And 7 Is

Words & Music by
Arthur Lee

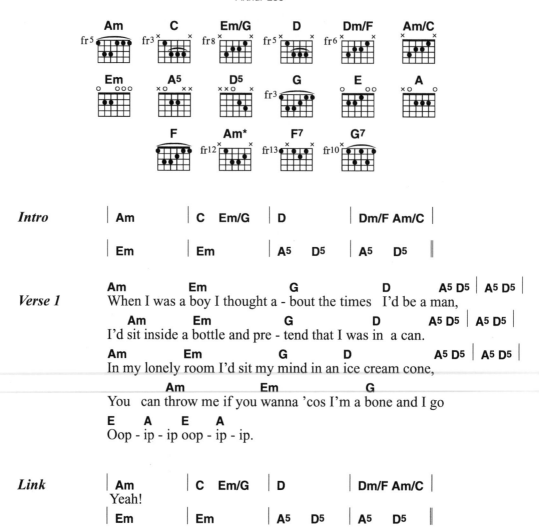

Intro

| Am | | C Em/G | D | | Dm/F Am/C |
| Em | | Em | A5 D5 | A5 D5 |

Verse 1

Am   Em   G   D   A5 D5 | A5 D5 |
When I was a boy I thought a - bout the times   I'd be a man,

        Am   Em   G   D   A5 D5 | A5 D5 |
I'd sit inside a bottle and pre - tend that I was in a can.

Am   Em   G   D   A5 D5 | A5 D5 |
In my lonely room I'd sit my mind in an ice cream cone,

                Am   Em   G
You   can throw me if you wanna 'cos I'm a bone and I go

E   A   E   A
Oop - ip - ip oop - ip - ip.

Link

| Am | | C Em/G | D | | Dm/F Am/C |
Yeah!
| Em | | Em | A5 D5 | A5 D5 |

Verse 2

```
      Am        Em           G                  D            A5 D5 | A5 D5 |
If I don't start cryin' it's be - cause that I have got no eyes,
        Am         Em           G     D            A5 D5 | A5 D5 |
My father's in the fireplace and my dog lies hypnotized.
Am              Em              G     D            A5 D5 | A5 D5 |
Through a crack of light I was un - able to find my way
Am              Em              G
Trapped inside a night but I'm a day and I go
E       A       E       A
Oop - ip - ip oop - ip - ip.
```

Link 2

As Link 1

```
| A5  D5 | A5  D5 | A5  D5 | A5  D5 |
  One,     two,     three,   four!
```

Instr

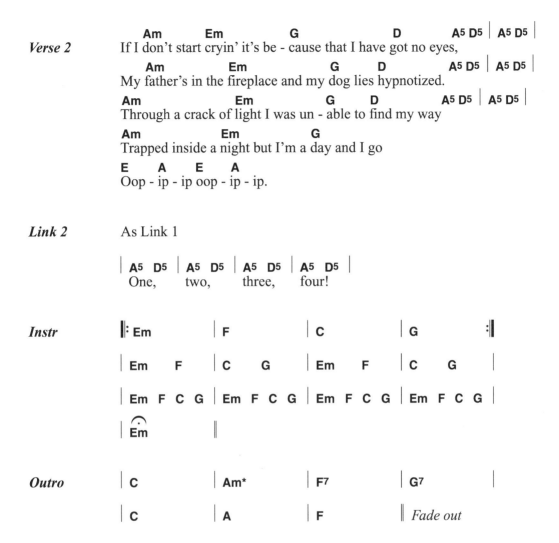

```
‖: Em        | F         | C         | G         :‖

| Em     F   | C     G   | Em     F   | C     G   |

| Em F C G | Em F C G | Em F C G | Em F C G |
    ⌢
| Em              ‖
```

Outro

```
| C         | Am*       | F7        | G7        |

| C         | A         | F         ‖ Fade out
```

MAGAZINE: Shot By Both Sides

Words & Music by
Peter Shelley & Howard Devoto

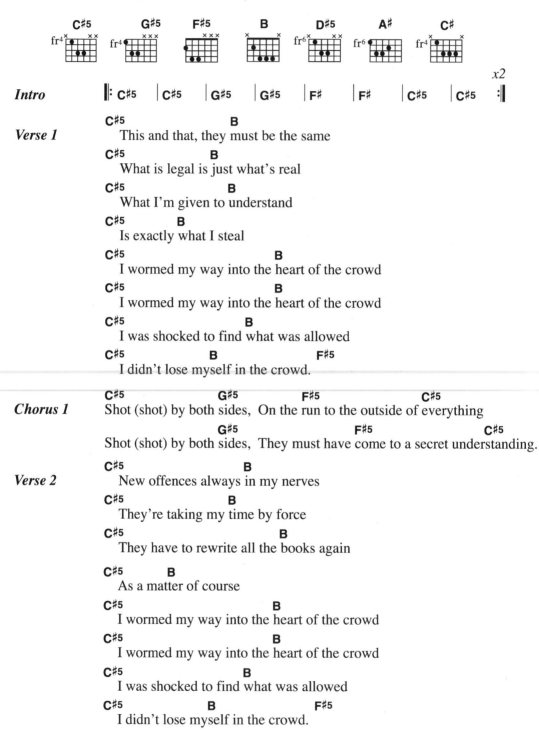

C#5 G#5 F#5 B D#5 A# C#

x2

Intro ‖: C#5 | C#5 | G#5 | G#5 | F# | F# | C#5 | C#5 :‖

Verse 1

C#5   B
This and that, they must be the same
C#5   B
What is legal is just what's real
C#5   B
What I'm given to understand
C#5   B
Is exactly what I steal
C#5   B
I wormed my way into the heart of the crowd
C#5   B
I wormed my way into the heart of the crowd
C#5   B
I was shocked to find what was allowed
C#5   B   F#5
I didn't lose myself in the crowd.

Chorus 1

C#5   G#5   F#5   C#5
Shot (shot) by both sides, On the run to the outside of everything
                       G#5   F#5   C#5
Shot (shot) by both sides, They must have come to a secret understanding.

Verse 2

C#5   B
New offences always in my nerves
C#5   B
They're taking my time by force
C#5   B
They have to rewrite all the books again
C#5   B
As a matter of course
C#5   B
I wormed my way into the heart of the crowd
C#5   B
I wormed my way into the heart of the crowd
C#5   B
I was shocked to find what was allowed
C#5   B   F#5
I didn't lose myself in the crowd.

Chorus 2

    C♯5   G♯5   F♯5   C♯5
Shot (shot) by both sides, On the run to the outside of everything
                           G♯5   F♯5   C♯5
Shot (shot) by both sides, They must have come to a secret understanding.

Instrumental

‖: D♯5 | D♯5 | A♯ | A♯ |
| G♯5 | G♯5 | D♯5 | D♯5 :‖ *x2*

Verse 3

C♯5   B
  'Why are you so edgy, Kid ?'
C♯5   B
  Asks the man with the voice
C♯5   B
  One thing follows another
C♯5   B
  You live and learn, you have no choice
C♯5   B
  I wormed my way into the heart of the crowd
C♯5   B
  I wormed my way into the heart of the crowd
C♯5   B
  I was shocked to find what was allowed
C♯5   B   F♯5
  I didn't lose myself in the crow-ow-ow-ow-ow-ow-ow . . .

Didn't lose myself in the crowd
Didn't lose myself in the crowd
I was shocked to find what was allowed
Didn't lose myself in the crowd,
But I wormed my way
But I wormed my way
But I wormed my way
But I wormed my way
But I wormed my way
But I wormed my way
But I wormed my way
But I wormed my way

Chorus 3

C♯5   G♯5   F♯5   C♯5
Shot (shot) by both sides, That old ass was doing the shooting
                         G♯5   F♯5   C♯5
Shot (shot) by both sides, We must have come to a secret understanding.

Outro

                        x4
‖: B | C♯ :‖

MERCURY REV: Holes

Words & Music by
Jonathan Donahue, Adam Snyder, David Fridmann & Sean Mackowiak

Verse 1

D   Bm
Time,

    F♯m G
All the long red lines,

    D Bm
That take con - trol

    F♯m   G
Of all the smokelike streams

    D   Bm
That flow into your dreams.

    F♯m G
That big blue open sea

    D   Bm
That can't be crossed,

    F♯m   G
That can't be climbed,

    D   Bm
Just born be - tween.

    F♯m G
Oh the two white lines,

    D   Bm
Distant gods and faded signs.

    F♯m G
Of all those blinking lights,

    D
You had to pick the one to - night.

Interlude   ‖: D | Bm | F♯m | G :‖ *Play 4 times*
(- night.)

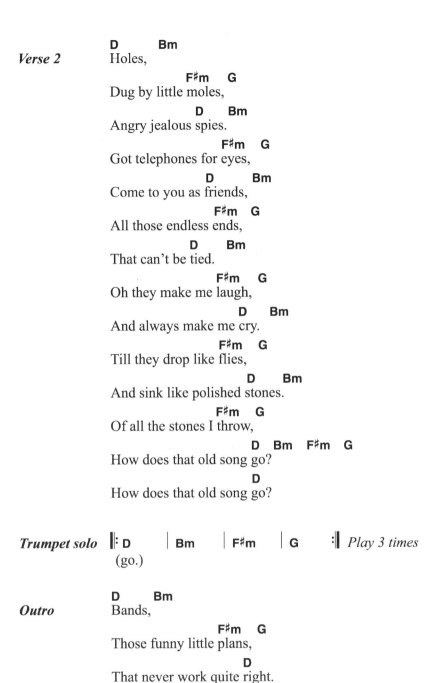

Verse 2

      D   **Bm**
Holes,

          F♯m   **G**
Dug by little moles,

        D   **Bm**
Angry jealous spies.

         F♯m   **G**
Got telephones for eyes,

        D   **Bm**
Come to you as friends,

       F♯m **G**
All those endless ends,

        D   **Bm**
That can't be tied.

         F♯m   **G**
Oh they make me laugh,

         D   **Bm**
And always make me cry.

        F♯m **G**
Till they drop like flies,

         D   **Bm**
And sink like polished stones.

       F♯m **G**
Of all the stones I throw,

        D **Bm** **F♯m** **G**
How does that old song go?

        D
How does that old song go?

Trumpet solo ‖: **D** | **Bm** | **F♯m** | **G**   :‖ *Play 3 times*
              (go.)

Outro

      D   **Bm**
Bands,

         F♯m **G**
Those funny little plans,

           D
That never work quite right.

THE MISSION: Tower Of Strength

Words by Wayne Hussey
Music by Craig Adams, Mick Brown, Simon Hinkler & Wayne Hussey

E5　C#m7　D6　F#11　E/G#　Aadd9　Em
B/E　G　A　Am　E/G#　C　G/B

Intro　| Drums　|

| E5　| C#m7　| D6　| F#11　E/G#　Aadd9　|

| E5　| C#m7　| D6　| F#11　D6　‖

Verse 1

E5　　　　　　C#m7
You raise me up,

D6　　　　　　F#11　E/G#　Aadd9
When I'm on the floor.

E5　　　　　　　C#m7
You see me through,

　　　　　D6
When I'm lonely and scared.

　　　F#11　　D6　E5　　　C#m7
And I'm feeling true to the written word

　　　　　D6
And you're true to me.

　　F#11　E/G#　Aadd9
And still I need　more

　　　　　E5　　　C#m7
It would tear me apart.

　　　D6　　　　F#11　D6
To feel no one ever cared.

Chorus 1

　　　　Em　| B/E　| Em
For me.

　　　　| B/E　| Em
For me.

　　　　| B/E　|
For me.

　　G　　　　A　　　　E5
You are a tower of strength to me.

Link 1　| (E5)　| C#m7　| D6　| F#11　E/G#　Aadd 9　‖

Verse 2

    E5   **C#m7**
You rescue me,

          D6
You are my faith.

My hope
    F#11 **E/G#** **Aadd9**
My liberty.

                      E5   **C#m7**
And when there is darkness all around,

          D6
You shine bright for me.

          F#11   **D6**
You are the guiding light.

Chorus 2

      Em | **B/E** | **Em**
To me.

            | **B/E** | **Em**
To me.

            | **B/E** |
To me.

     G   **A**   **(E5)**
You are a tower of strength to me.

Link 2

| **(E5)** | **C#m7** | **D6** | **F#11** **E/G#** **Aadd 9** ‖

Instr.

‖: **Am** **E/G#** | **C**   **G/B** | **Am** **E/G#** | **C**   **G/B** :‖

Link 3

| **(E5)** | **C#m7** | **D6** | **F#11** **E/G#** **Aadd 9** ‖

| **(E5)** | **C#m7** | **D6** | **F#11**   **D6**   ‖

Verse 3

            E5   **C#m7**
You are all passion and heart,

          D6   **F#11** **E/G#** **Aadd9**
When I lay in your embrace.

        E5   **C#m7**
And heaven is in your kiss,

        D6   **F#11**   **D6**
Sal - vation lies just a touch away.

Chorus 3   As Chorus 1

Outro

‖: **(E5)** | **C#m7** | **D6** | **F#11** **E/G#** **Aadd 9** |

| **(E5)** | **C#m7** | **D6** | **F#11**   **D6**   :‖ *Repeat to fade*

MISSION OF BURMA:
That's When I Reach For My Revolver

Words & Music by
Clint Conley

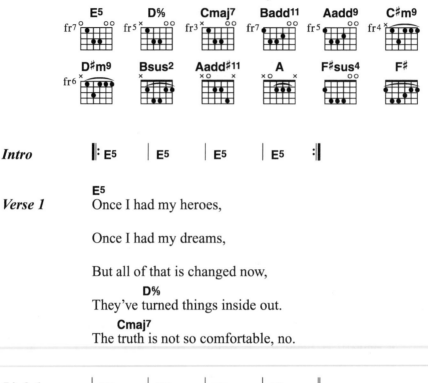

Intro ‖: E5 | E5 | E5 | E5 :‖

Verse 1

E5
Once I had my heroes,

Once I had my dreams,

But all of that is changed now,
D%
They've turned things inside out.
Cmaj7
The truth is not so comfortable, no.

Link 1 | E5 | E5 | E5 | E5 |

Verse 2

E5
And mother taught us patience,

The virtues of restraint.

And father taught us boundaries,
D%
Be - yond which we must go.
Cmaj7
To find the secrets promised us, yeah.

Link 2 | E5 | E5 | E5 | E5 |

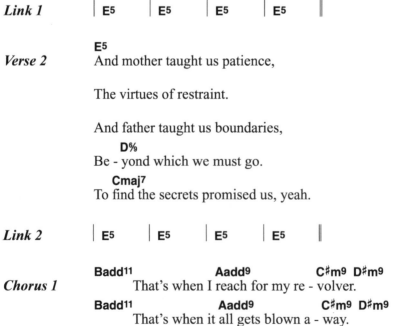

Chorus 1

Badd11   Aadd9   C#m9 D#m9
   That's when I reach for my re - volver.
Badd11   Aadd9   C#m9 D#m9
   That's when it all gets blown a - way.

Badd11   **Aadd9**   **C♯m9 D♯m9**
That's when I reach for my re - volver.
Badd11   **Aadd9**   **C♯m9**
The spirit fights to find its way.

Link 3 | **E5** | **E5** | **E5** | **E5** ||

Verse 3 **E5**
A friend of mine once told me,

His one and only aim.

To build a giant castle,
  D%
And live inside his name.
Cmaj7
Cry and whispers sing in muted pain.

Link 4 | **E5** | **E5** | **E5** | **E5** ||

Chorus 2 As Chorus 1

Solo ‖: **C♯m9** | **C♯m9** | **Bsus2** | **Bsus2** :‖

  ‖: **Aadd♯11 A Aadd♯11** | **A Aadd♯11 A** | **F♯sus4 F♯** | **F♯** :‖

  | **E5** | **E5** | **E5** | **E5** ||

Bridge **E5**
Tonight the sky is empty,

But that is nothing new.

Its dead eyes look upon us,
   D%   **Cmaj7**
And they tell me we're nothing but slaves.

Chorus 3 ‖: **Badd11**   **Aadd9**   **C♯m9 D♯m9**
That's when I reach for my re - volver.
Badd11   **Aadd9**   **C♯m9 D♯m9**
That's when I reach for my re - volver. :‖
Badd11   **Aadd9**   **C♯m9 D♯m9**
That's when I reach for my re - volver.
Badd11   **Aadd9**   **C♯m9**
That's when I reach for my re - volver.

Outro | **C♯m9** | **C♯m9** | **C♯m9** ||

MODEST MOUSE: Float On

Words & Music by
Isaac Brock, Dann Gallucci & Eric Judy

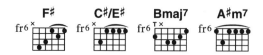

Intro   ‖: F♯ | C♯/E♯ | Bmaj7 | A♯m7 :‖

Verse 1

F♯   C♯/E♯   Bmaj7
I backed my car into a cop car the other day,
   A♯m7   F♯
Well he just drove off, sometimes life's ok.
                    C♯/E♯   Bmaj7
I ran my mouth off a bit too much, oh what can I say,
   A♯m7
Well you just laughed it off, it was all ok.

Link 1 | F♯ | C♯/E♯ | Bmaj7 | A♯m7   ‖

Chorus 1

F♯   C♯/E♯   Bmaj7
And we'll all float on ok.
          A♯m7   F♯
And we'll all float on ok.
          C♯/E♯   Bmaj7
And we'll all float on ok.
          A♯m7
And we'll all float on anyway. Well

Verse 2

      F♯   C♯/E♯   Bmaj7
(Well,) a fake Jamaican took every last dime with a scam,
   A♯m7   F♯
It was worth it just to learn some sleight-of-hand.
                            C♯/E♯   Bmaj7
Bad news comes, don't you worry   even when it lands,
   A♯m7   F♯
Good news will work its way to all them plans.
                    C♯/E♯   Bmaj7
We both got fired on the exactly the same day,
   A♯m7
Well we'll float on, good news is on the way.

Link 2 | F♯ | C♯/E♯ | Bmaj⁷ | A♯m⁷ ‖

Chorus 2

F♯   C♯/E♯   Bmaj⁷
And we'll all float on ok.

     A♯m⁷   F♯
And we'll all float on ok.

     C♯/E♯   Bmaj⁷
And we'll all float on ok.

     A♯m⁷   F♯
And we'll all float on, al - right.

     C♯/E♯
Already we'll all float on,

  Bmaj⁷   A♯m⁷   F♯
Now don't you worry, we'll all float on, al - right.

     C♯/E♯   Bmaj⁷
Already, we'll all float on, al - right.

     A♯m⁷
Don't worry, we'll all float on.

Link 3 | N.C. | N.C. | N.C. | N.C. ‖

Verse 3

F♯
Alright, already,

     C♯/E♯   Bmaj⁷
And we'll all float on, al - right.

     A♯m⁷   F♯
Already, we'll all float on, al - right.

     C♯/E♯   Bmaj⁷
Don't worry even if things end up a bit to heavy,

     A♯m⁷   F♯
We'll all float on, al - right.

     C♯/E♯   Bmaj⁷
Already, we'll all float on, al - right

     A♯m⁷   F♯
Already, we'll all float on, ok.

     C♯/E♯
Don't worry, we'll all float on.

  Bmaj⁷   A♯m⁷   F♯
Even if things get heavy we'll all float on, al - right.

N.C.
Already, we'll all float on.

Don't you worry, we'll all float on,

We'll all float on.

MINISTRY: Jesus Built My Hotrod

Words & Music by
Gibby Haynes, Al Jourgensen, William Rieflin & Michael Balch

B5/F **B♭5/F** **D5** **F5**

(N.C.)

Intro
Soon I discovered that this rock thing was true
Jerry Lee Lewis was the devil
Jesus was an architect previous to his career as a prophet
All of a sudden, i found myself in love with the world
So there was only one thing that i could do
Was ding a-ding dang my dang a-long ling long

‖: B5/F B♭5/F │ B5/F (F) :‖ *Play 8 times (riff cont. sim.)*

(F)

Verse 1
Ding dang a-dong bong bing bong,
Ticky ticky son-of-a-gun.
Everytime I try to do it all now baby,
Am I on the run.
Why why why why why baby,
If it's so evil then.
Give me my time, with all my power,
Give it to me all again, wow.
Ding a ding a dang a dong dong ding dong,
Every where I go.

D5

Chorus 1
Everytime you tell me baby,
When I settle down.
Got to get me a trailer park,
And hold my world around.
Why why why why.

(F)

Verse 2
Ding ding donga dong dong ding dong,
Dingy dingy son of a gun.
Half my time I tell you baby,
Never am I all for sure.
Why why why why why baby,
Sicky sicky from within.
Everytime I stick my finger on in ya,
You're a wild wild little town bitch.
Now how 'bout ding a dang dong dong dong ling long,
Dingy a dingy dong a down.

Chorus 2   As Chorus 1

Verse 3

(F)
In my dang a ding a ding a ding dong,
A sticky sticky son of a gun.
Ding a danga danga dong dong ding dong,
Why why never know.
Why why wack a dong a dang ding dong,
Then you take it on the bill.
Ding dang dong don't dong, whoa.

| D5 | D5 | |

N.C
I wanna love ya.

Solo 1

‖: B5/F B♭5/F | B5/F (F) :‖ *Play 3 times*

‖: D5 | D5 :‖ *Play 3 times*

Verse 4

(F)
Why why why, why why darling,
Do you do you tell me to play.
Half the time I talk about it all now baby,
You know what I'm talkin' about I said.
Why why why it'll,
Ticky ticky ticky ticky,
Son of a gun.
Ding ding dong a bong bong bing bong,
Ticky ticky thought of a gun.

Bridge

N.C.
Bing bing bang a bang a bang bing bong bing a bing bang a bong,
F5 N.C.
Binga bing a bang a bong bong bing bong bing banga bong.
F5 N.C.
Bing bing bang a bong bong bing bing binga binga banga bong,
F5 N.C.
Bing bing bang a bang bang bing bong, Ah.

Solo 2

‖: (F) B5/F | B♭5/F B5/F | (F) :‖ *Play 10 times*

| D5 | D5 | D5 | D5 | |

| N.C. | ‖: B5/F B♭5/F | B5/F (F) :‖ *Play 6 times*

Verse 5

(F)
Ding dang a dang bong bing bong,
Ticky ticky thought of a gun..
Everytime I try to do it all now baby,
Am I on the run.
Why why why,
It'll ticky ticky ticky ticky ticky ticky,
Dawn of a gun.
Bing bing bang a bong a bong bing bang a,
Ticky ticky thought of a gun.
Bing bip bip a bop bop boom bam,
Ticky ticky through the day.
If you got a doubt 'bout baby,
The memory is on the bed.
Why why why why why,
Darlin' uh it don't know.
When my time is on,
Might tell me never do it on his own.
If my time was all as is yours,
Make me burn a wish.
When my time with you is brutish,
No I'll never not ever.
Why why why why why why baby heavy hell.
Alone and it's here it's this thunder,
The thunder oh thunder, Oh.

Outro

‖: (F) B5/F	Bb5/F B5/F	(F)	:‖ *Play 3 times*
D5	D5	D5	

N.C.
Jesus built my car,
It's a love affair,
Mainly Jesus and my hotrod. (Yeah, Fuck it.)

MOGWAI: Cody

Words & Music by
Stuart Braithwaite

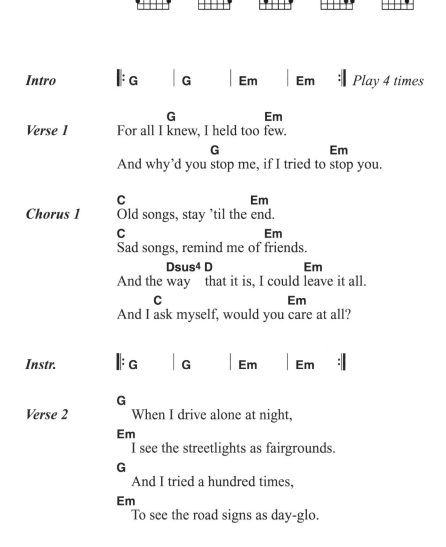

Intro ‖: G | G | Em | Em :‖ *Play 4 times*

Verse 1
         G   Em
For all I knew, I held too few.
                 G   Em
And why'd you stop me, if I tried to stop you.

Chorus 1
C   Em
Old songs, stay 'til the end.
C   Em
Sad songs, remind me of friends.
          Dsus4 D   Em
And the way   that it is, I could leave it all.
          C   Em
And I ask myself, would you care at all?

Instr. ‖: G | G | Em | Em :‖

Verse 2
G
    When I drive alone at night,
Em
    I see the streetlights as fairgrounds.
G
    And I tried a hundred times,
Em
    To see the road signs as day-glo.

Chorus 2   As Chorus 1

Solo ‖: G | G | Em | Em :‖ *Play 4 times*

Chorus 3   As Chorus 1

MUDHONEY: Touch Me I'm Sick

Words & Music by
Mark Arm, Steve Turner, Matt Lukin & Dan Peters

G#5   D5   C#5   B5   F#5   D#5

Intro   ‖: G#5 D5 C#5 B5 F#5 | G#5 D5 C#5 B5 :‖ *Play 4 times*

Verse 1
G#5   D5 C#5 B5   F#5 | G#5 D5 C#5 B5 |
Well, I've been bad,
G#5   D5 C#5 B5   F#5 | G#5 D5 C#5 B5 |
And I've been worse.
G#5   D5 C#5 B5   F#5 | G#5 D5 C#5 B5 |
And I'm a   creep,
G#5   D5 C#5 B5   F#5 | G#5 D5 C#5 B5 |
And I'm a   jerk.

Chorus 1   Come on,
C#5 B5
Touch me, I'm sick.

Link   ‖: G#5 D5 C#5 B5 F#5 | G#5 D5 C#5 B5 :‖

Verse 2
G#5 D5   C#5 B5   F#5 | G#5 D5 C#5 B5 |
I won't live long,
G#5   D5 C#5 B5 F#5 | G#5 D5 C#5 B5 |
And I'm full of rot.
G#5   D5 C#5 B5 F#5 | G#5 D5 C#5 B5 |
Gonna give you, girl,
G#5   D5   C#5 B5 F#5 | G#5 D5 C#5 B5 |
Every - thing I   got.

Chorus 2
C#5 B5
Touch me, I'm sick,

| G#5 D5 C#5 B5 F#5 | G#5 D5 C#5 B5 |
C#5 B5
Touch me, I'm sick,

‖: G#5 D5 C#5 B5 F#5 | G#5 D5 C#5 B5 :‖

Bridge 1

G#5   C#5
 Come on baby, now come with me,
D#5   C#5
If you don't come,
D#5   C#5
If you don't come,
D#5   C#5
If you don't come,
   D#5   C#5
You'll die alone.

Solo

𝄆 G#5 | G#5   𝄇

𝄆 G#5 D5 C#5 B5 F#5 | G#5 D5 C#5 B5 𝄇 *Play 4 times*

Verse 3

G#5 D5 C#5 B5 F#5 | G#5 D5 C#5 B5
 I'm dis - eased,
G#5 D5 C#5 B5 F#5 | G#5 D5 C#5 B5
 And I don't mind.
G#5 D5 C#5 B5 F#5 | G#5 D5 C#5 B5
 I'll make you love me,
G#5   D5 C#5 B5 F#5 | G#5 D5 C#5 B5
 'Till the day you die.

Chorus 3

Come on,
C#5 B5
   Touch me, I'm sick.

| G#5 D5 C#5 B5 F#5 | G#5 D5 C#5 B5 |
C#5 B5
   Fuck me, I'm sick.

| G#5 D5 C#5 B5 F#5 | G#5 D5 C#5 B5 |

Outro

G#5   C#5
 Come on baby, now come with me,
D#5   C#5
If you don't come,
D#5   C#5
If you don't come,
D#5   C#5
If you don't come,
   D#5   C#5 G#5
You'll die alone.

THE NEW YORK DOLLS: Personality Crisis

Words & Music by
David Johansen & Johnny Thunders

C5   D5   G5   C   Csus4   Dsus4   D   G

Intro | C5 | D5 | G5 | G5 |

‖: C Csus4 C | D Dsus4 D | G | G   *x3* :‖

Verse 1

       G
Well, we can't take her this week

And her friends don't want another speech
C   Csus4 C   D
Hopin' for her that   someday
     Dsus4 D   G
They'll hear   what she's gotta say.

Chorus 1

          C Csus4 C   D   Dsus4
All about that personality   crisis
       D   G
You got it while it was hot
       C Csus4 C   D   Dsus4 D   G
But now frustration and heartache is what you've got
                  C   Csus4 C D Dsus4
You know I'm talkin' 'bout her personali - ty.

| C Csus4 C | D Dsus4 D | G | G |

Verse 2

      G
Well, now you're tryin' to be someone, now you gotta do something

Wanna be someone who cou-ou-ounts
            C   Csus4 C   D   Dsus4   D   G
But you're thinkin' 'bout the   times you did, they took every ounce
         C   Csus4   C D   Dsus4 D   G
Well, it sure gotta be a shame when you start to scream and shout.

      C Csus4 C   D Dsus4 D G

cont.   You gotta contradict all those times you butterflied about

    You was butterflyin'.

       C Csus4 C D

Chorus 2 About a personality crisis

       D   G

    You got it while it was hot

    It's always hot, you know,

      C Csus4 C D   Dsus4 D G

    But frustration and heartache is what you've got

             C Csus4 C D Dsus4

    I'm tryin' to talk about personality

       G

    Yeah, yeah, yeah! Ow!

Instrumental | **C Csus4 C** | **D Dsus4 D** | **G** | **G** |

       | **C Csus4 C** | **D Dsus4 D** | **G** | **(G)** |

        C Csus4 C   D Dsus4 D G

Link   And you're a prima-ballerina on a spring aft - ernoon

    C   Csus4   D Dsus4 D   G

    Change on into the wolf-man, howlin' at the moon.

    (Aoooh!)

       C Csus4 C D

Chorus 3 About a personality crisis

       D   G

    You got it while it was hot

    It's always hot, you know

      C Csus4 C D   Dsus4 D G

    But frustration and heartache is what you've got

            C   Csus4 C D Dsus4 D

    I, I'm talking 'bout a persa-personality.

    | **G** | **G** | **C Csus4 C** | **D Dsus4 D** | **G** | **G** |

Verse 3

              G
Now, with all the cards of fate that mother nature sends

Your mirror's gettin' jammed up with all your friends

      C   **Csus⁴ C D**   **Dsus⁴ D G**
That's person - al - ity, every scene is startin' to blend

C   **Csus⁴ C D**   **Dsus⁴**   **D**   **G**
Person - al - ity, when your mind starts to bend

             C   **Csus⁴ C D**   **Dsus⁴**   **D G**
Got so much person - al - ity, flashin' of a friend, of a friend

Of a friend, of a friend, of a friend

C   **Csus⁴ C D**   **Dsus⁴**   **D**   **G**
Person - al - ity, wonderin' how celebrities ever mend,

Looking fine on television.

Chorus 4

C   **Csus⁴ C D**   **Dsus⁴**
Person - al - ity crisis

      D   **G**
You got it while it was hot

                  C Csus⁴ C   **D**   **Dsus⁴ D**   **G**
It's always hot, you know, but frustration and heartache is all you've got

                 C   **Csus⁴ C D**   **Dsus⁴ D**   **G**
Don't you worry, it's just a person - al - ity crisis, please don't cry

          C   **Csus⁴ C D**   **Dsus⁴ D**   **G**
It's just a person - al - ity crisis, please don't stop

            C   **Csus⁴ C D**
Because you walk a person - al - ity, talk a

Dsus⁴ D   **Dsus⁴ D**   **G**
Per - son - al - i - ty.

NIRVANA: Where Did You Sleep Last Night

Words & Music by
Huddie Ledbetter

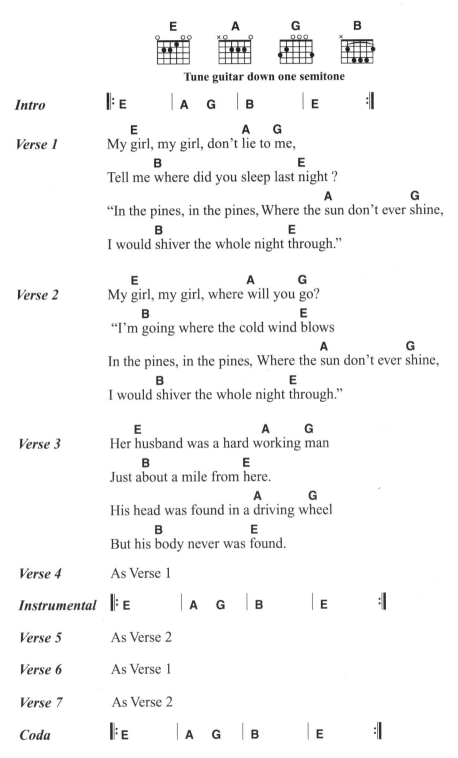

Tune guitar down one semitone

Intro

‖: E | A G | B | E :‖

Verse 1

    E   A   G
My girl, my girl, don't lie to me,
         B   E
Tell me where did you sleep last night ?
                                  A   G
"In the pines, in the pines, Where the sun don't ever shine,
         B   E
I would shiver the whole night through."

Verse 2

    E   A   G
My girl, my girl, where will you go?
        B   E
"I'm going where the cold wind blows
                             A   G
In the pines, in the pines, Where the sun don't ever shine,
         B   E
I would shiver the whole night through."

Verse 3

    E   A   G
Her husband was a hard working man
        B   E
Just about a mile from here.
                 A   G
His head was found in a driving wheel
        B   E
But his body never was found.

Verse 4

As Verse 1

Instrumental

‖: E | A G | B | E :‖

Verse 5

As Verse 2

Verse 6

As Verse 1

Verse 7

As Verse 2

Coda

‖: E | A G | B | E :‖

NINE INCH NAILS: Hurt

Words & Music by
Trent Reznor

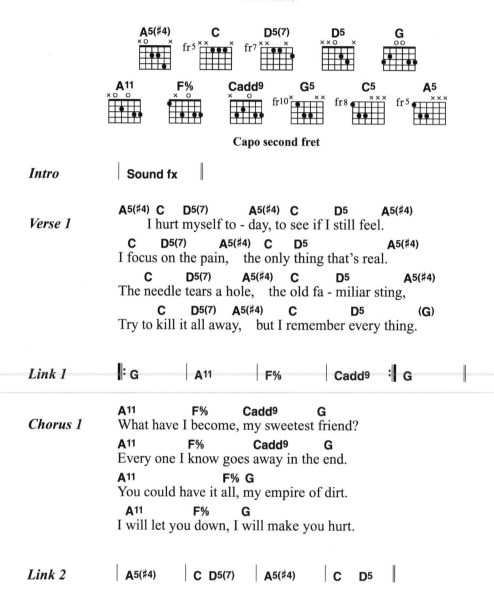

Capo second fret

Intro | Sound fx ‖

Verse 1

A5(♯4) C   D5(7)   A5(♯4) C   D5   A5(♯4)
    I hurt myself to - day, to see if I still feel.

  C   D5(7)   A5(♯4) C   D5   A5(♯4)
I focus on the pain,   the only thing that's real.

    C   D5(7)   A5(♯4) C   D5   A5(♯4)
The needle tears a hole,   the old fa - miliar sting,

    C   D5(7) A5(♯4)   C   D5   (G)
Try to kill it all away,   but I remember every thing.

Link 1 ‖: G | A11 | F‰ | Cadd9 :‖ G   ‖

Chorus 1

A11   F‰   Cadd9   G
What have I become, my sweetest friend?

A11   F‰   Cadd9   G
Every one I know goes away in the end.

A11   F‰ G
You could have it all, my empire of dirt.

  A11   F‰   G
I will let you down, I will make you hurt.

Link 2 | A5(♯4) | C D5(7) | A5(♯4) | C   D5 ‖

Verse 2

A5(♯4) C   D5(7)   A5(♯4)   C   D5   A5(♯4)
I wear this crown of shit, up - on my liars chair,

C   D5(7)   A5(♯4)   C   D5   A5(♯4)
Full of broken thoughts,   I can now repair,

      C   D5(7) A5(♯4)   C   D5   A5(♯4)
Be - neath this state of time, the feel - ings dis - appear

        C   D5(7)   A5(♯4) C D5   G
You are someone else,   I am still right here.

Chorus 2

A11   F‰   Cadd9   G
What have I become, my sweetest friend?

A11   F‰   Cadd9   G
Every one I know goes away in the end.

    A11   F‰   G
And you could have it all, my empire of dirt.

    A11   F‰   G
I will let you down, I will make you hurt.

    A11   F‰   G
If I could start again, a mil - lion miles away

    A11   F‰   G5   C5   A5
I would keep myself, I would find a way.

Outro | **Sound fx** ‖

THE ONLY ONES:
Another Girl, Another Planet

Words & Music by
Peter Perrett

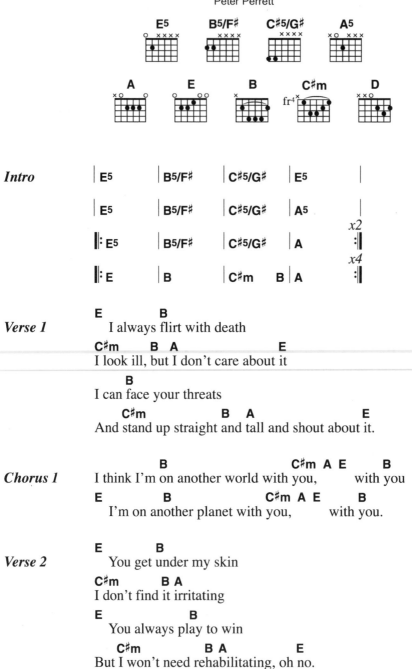

Intro

| E5 | B5/F♯ | C♯5/G♯ | E5 | |

| E5 | B5/F♯ | C♯5/G♯ | A5 | |

x2

‖: E5 | B5/F♯ | C♯5/G♯ | A :‖

x4

‖: E | B | C♯m B | A :‖

Verse 1

   E   B
  I always flirt with death
C♯m   B A   E
I look ill, but I don't care about it

     B
I can face your threats
    C♯m   B A   E
And stand up straight and tall and shout about it.

Chorus 1

           B   C♯m A E   B
I think I'm on another world with you,   with you
E   B   C♯m A E   B
  I'm on another planet with you,   with you.

Verse 2

   E   B
  You get under my skin
C♯m   B A
I don't find it irritating
E   B
  You always play to win
   C♯m   B A   E
But I won't need rehabilitating, oh no.

Chorus 2

                B   **C♯m A E**   **B**
I think I'm on another world with you,   with you

E   **B**   **C♯m A E**   **B**
  I'm on another planet with you,   with you.

Bridge

  E   **A**   **E**   **A**
  Another girl, another planet

  E   **B**   **D**   **A**
  Another girl, another planet.

Guitar Solo

                                       x6
‖: **E** | **B** | **C♯m** **B** | **A**   :‖

Verse 3

  E   **B**
  Space travel's in my blood

C♯m   **B**   **A**   **E**
There ain't nothing I can do about it.

              B
Long journeys wear me out

   C♯m   **B**   **A**   **E**
But   I know I can't live without it, I know

Chorus 3

                B   **C♯m A E**   **B**
I think I'm on another world with you,   with you

E   **B**   **C♯m A E**   **B**
  I'm on another planet with you,   with you.

Outro

  E   **B** **C♯m** **B** **E**   **A**
  Another girl   is loving you now

  E   **B**   **C♯m** **B**   **C♯m A**
  Another planet,   is   holding you down

  D   **B**   **E**
  Another planet.

GRAM PARSONS:
Return Of The Grievious Angel

Words & Music by
Gram Parsons & Beau Brown

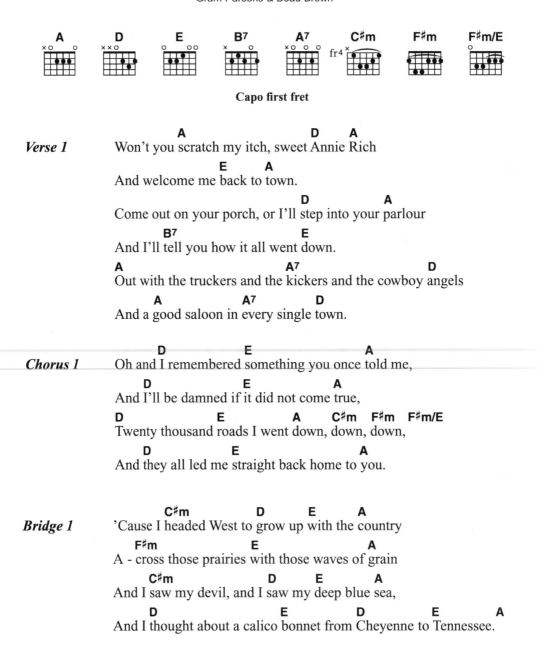

Capo first fret

Verse 1

        A   **D**   **A**
Won't you scratch my itch, sweet Annie Rich
               E   **A**
And welcome me back to town.
                          D   **A**
Come out on your porch, or I'll step into your parlour
    B⁷   **E**
And I'll tell you how it all went down.
A   **A⁷**   **D**
Out with the truckers and the kickers and the cowboy angels
     A   **A⁷**   **D**
And a good saloon in every single town.

Chorus 1

       D   **E**   **A**
Oh and I remembered something you once told me,
    D   **E**   **A**
And I'll be damned if it did not come true,
D   **E**   **A** **C♯m** **F♯m** **F♯m/E**
Twenty thousand roads I went down, down, down,
    D   **E**   **A**
And they all led me straight back home to you.

Bridge 1

     C♯m   **D**   **E**   **A**
'Cause I headed West to grow up with the country
F♯m   **E**   **A**
A - cross those prairies with those waves of grain
  C♯m   **D**   **E**   **A**
And I saw my devil, and I saw my deep blue sea,
    D   **E**   **D**   **E**   **A**
And I thought about a calico bonnet from Cheyenne to Tennessee.

Verse 2

```
                    D   A
We flew straight across that river bridge,
         E      A
Last night, half past two
                         D              A
The switchman wave his lantern goodbye and good day
   B7          E
As we went rollin' through.
A                      A7           D
Billboards and truckstops pass by the grievous angel,
    A          E       A
And now I know just what I have to do.
```

Instrumental

```
| A  | D  A | A  E | A  | A  | D  A | B7 | E  |

| A  | A  A7 | D  | D  | A  | E  | A  | A  ||
```

Bridge 2

```
      C#m          D      E   A
And the man on the radio won't leave me a - lone
      F#m          E                        A
He wants to take my money for something that I've never been shown.
      C#m          D     E   A
And I saw my devil,  and I saw my deep blue sea,
    D              E        D      E      A
And I thought about a calico bonnet from Cheyenne to Tennessee.
```

Verse 3

```
                       D       A
The news I could bring I met up with the King
           E      A
On his head an am - phetamine crown.
                       D     A
He talked about unbuckling that old Bible belt
      B7               E
And lighted out for some desert town.
A                      A7               D
Out with the truckers and the kickers and the cowboy angels,
   A         A7        D
And a good saloon in every single town.
```

Chorus 2

```
     D          E           A
Oh, but I remembered something you once told me,
   D        E       A
And I'll be damned if it did not come true.
D          E        A    C#m F#m
Twenty thousand roads I went down, down, down,
   D        E            A
And they all led me straight back home to you.
D          E        A    C#m F#m  F#m/E
Twenty thousand roads I went down, down, down,
   D        E              A   E A
And they all led me straight back home to you.
```

PAVEMENT: Cut Your Hair

Words & Music by
Stephen Malkmus

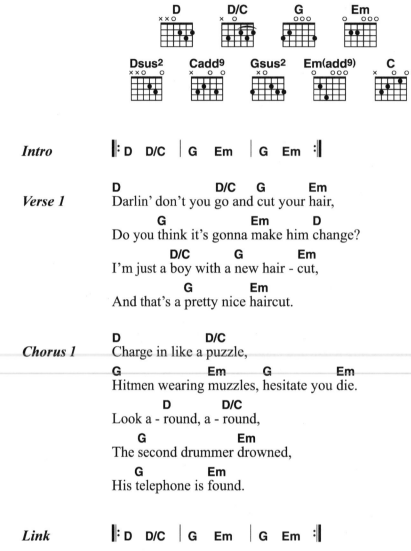

Intro   ‖: D D/C │ G Em │ G Em :‖

Verse 1

D   D/C G   Em
Darlin' don't you go and cut your hair,

        G   Em   D
Do you think it's gonna make him change?

              D/C   G   Em
I'm just a boy with a new hair - cut,

          G   Em
And that's a pretty nice haircut.

Chorus 1

D   D/C
Charge in like a puzzle,

G   Em   G   Em
Hitmen wearing muzzles, hesitate you die.

            D   D/C
Look a - round, a - round,

      G   Em
The second drummer drowned,

       G   Em
His telephone is found.

Link   ‖: D D/C │ G Em │ G Em :‖

Verse 2

```
D                 D/C
Music scene is crazy,

G        Em  G       Em   D
Bands start up   each and every day.
              D/C    G           Em
I saw an - other one just the other day,
    G           Em
A special new band.
```

Chorus 2

```
D             D/C    G               Em
I remember lying, I don't remember a lie,
  G               Em
I don't remember a word.
      D             D/C   G           Em
But I don't care, I care, I really don't care,
        G                 Em
Did you see the drummer's hair?
```

Link

‖: D   D/C │ G   Em │ G   Em :‖   *Play 6 times*

Solo

‖: D   D/C │ G   Em │ G   Em :‖

Verse 3

```
D               D/C     G       Em
Advertising looks and chops a must.
G       Em
No big hair.
D               D/C       G       Em
Songs mean a lot, when songs are bought,
      G       Em
And so are you.
D         D/C         G       Em
Let's run down to the practice room,
      G           Em
At - tention and fame.
        D         D/C     G       Em     G       Em
A ca - reer, ca - reer, ca - reer, ca - reer, ca - reer, ca - reer.
```

Outro

‖: D   D/C │ G   Em │ G   Em :‖

│ Dsus2 Cadd9 │ Gsus2 Emadd9 │

│ Gsus2 Emadd9 │ C   ‖

PINK FLOYD: See Emily Play

Words & Music by
Syd Barrett

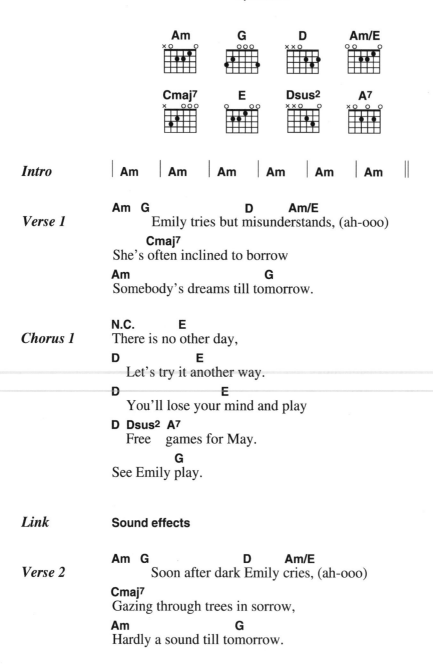

Intro | Am | Am | Am | Am | Am | Am ||

Verse 1
Am G   D   Am/E
    Emily tries but misunderstands, (ah-ooo)
Cmaj⁷
She's often inclined to borrow
Am   G
Somebody's dreams till tomorrow.

Chorus 1
N.C.   E
There is no other day,
D   E
    Let's try it another way.
D   E
    You'll lose your mind and play
D Dsus² A⁷
   Free   games for May.
             G
See Emily play.

Link   **Sound effects**

Verse 2
Am G   D   Am/E
    Soon after dark Emily cries, (ah-ooo)
Cmaj⁷
Gazing through trees in sorrow,
Am   G
Hardly a sound till tomorrow.

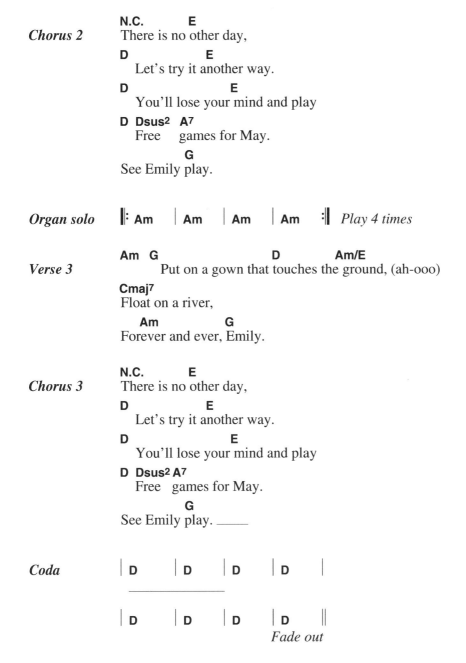

Chorus 2

N.C.   E
There is no other day,

D   E
  Let's try it another way.

D   E
  You'll lose your mind and play

D Dsus2 A7
  Free   games for May.

           G
See Emily play.

Organ solo

‖: Am | Am | Am | Am :‖ *Play 4 times*

Verse 3

Am G   D   Am/E
        Put on a gown that touches the ground, (ah-ooo)

Cmaj7
Float on a river,

   Am   G
Forever and ever, Emily.

Chorus 3

N.C.   E
There is no other day,

D   E
  Let's try it another way.

D   E
  You'll lose your mind and play

D Dsus2 A7
  Free   games for May.

           G
See Emily play. _____

Coda

| D | D | D | D |

_____

| D | D | D | D ‖
                Fade out

THE PIXIES: Debaser

Words & Music by
Charles Thompson

Intro

bass only

| B♭ F | C F | Dm Am | B♭ C ‖

‖: *(F) (B♭) | (C) (Dm) | (Am) (B♭) | (F) (C) :‖
*implied

Verse 1

F   B♭   G
Got me a movie

  B♭   F
I want you to know

  B♭   G
Slicing up eyeballs

  B♭   F
I want you to know

  B♭   G
Girlie so groovy

  B♭   F
I want you to know

     B♭   G
Don't know about you

    B♭ F   G
But I am un chien Andalusia

  B♭   F   B♭   G
I am un chien Anda - lusia

  B♭   F   B♭   G
I am un chien Anda - lusia

  B♭   F   B♭   G
I am un chien Anda - lusia

       B♭
Wanna grow up to be,

               F C F
Be a debaser, debaser,

Dm Am B♭   **C**
Deba - ser, debaser.

Link 1   ‖: *(F) (B♭) | (C) (Dm) | (Am) (B♭) | (F) (C) :‖
               Debaser.   Debaser.

Verse 2

F   B♭   G
Got me a movie

   B♭   F
A - ha ha ha ho

B♭   G
Slicing up eyeballs

   B♭   F
A - ha ha ha ho

B♭   G
Girlie so groovie

   B♭   F
A - ha ha ha ho

     B♭   G
Don't know about you

   B♭ F   G
But I am un chien Andalusia

  B♭   F   B♭   G
I am un chien Anda - lusia

  B♭   F   B♭   G
I am un chien Anda - lusia

  B♭   F   B♭   G   B♭
I am un chien Anda - lusia

| F   C | F | Dm Am | B♭   C ‖
       (Debaser.)   Debaser.   (Debaser.)

Link 2   ‖: *(F) (B♭) | (C) (Dm) | (Am) (B♭) | (F) (C) :‖
               Debaser.   (Debaser.)   Debaser.   (Debaser.)

Outro   ‖: F   B♭ | G   B♭ | F   B♭ | G   B♭ :‖   *Play 4 times*
        Debaser. *(1° only)*

  ⌢
| F   ‖

QUEENS OF THE STONE AGE: No One Knows

Words & Music by
Josh Homme, Nick Oliveri & Mark Lanegan

Em/B   Em   B   E♭   B5   C5   E♭5 (D#5)

A5   Em*   F#7/E   Em/G   Edim   D5

Tuning (from bottom string): C F B♭ E♭ G C

Intro

| Em/B | Em/B | Em | Em | Em |

| Em | Em | Em | Em | Em |

Verse 1

Em
   We get some rules to follow

That and this,
                 B
These and those
E♭ | Em | Em | Em |Em |
   No one knows.

Verse 2

Em
   We get these pills to swallow
                      B
How they stick in your throat
E♭ | Em | Em | Em |
   Tastes like gold.
Em   B
   Oh what you do to me
E♭   Em
   No one knows.

Chorus 1

N.C.   B5
I realise you're mine
   N.C.   B5
Indeed a fool of mine
   N.C.   B5
I realise you're mine
   N.C.   B5
Indeed a fool am I, ah._____

Link

| Em | Em | Em | Em |

Link | Em | Em | Em | Em |

Verse 3

Em
  I journey through the desert

                B
Of the mind with no hope

E♭   Em
  I follow.

Verse 4

Em
  I drift along the ocean

              B
Dead lifeboats in the sun

E♭   Em
  And come undone.

          B
Pleasantly caving in

E♭   Em
  I come undone.

Chorus 2   As Chorus 1

Interlude

                                          x2
‖: E5 | E5 | E5 | B5 C5 E♭5 B5 A5 B5 :‖

                       x3
‖: B5 C5 E♭5 B5 A5 B5 :‖

Bass solo | N.C. (E5) | (E5) | (E5) | (E5) |

Guitar solo

| Em* | Em* | A5 | B5 | Em* | F♯7/E |

| Em/G | Edim | Em* | F♯7/E | D5 | D♯5 |

Bass | E* (bass) | E* (bass) | E* (bass) | E* (bass) |

Verse 5

E* (bass)
  Heaven smiles above me

Em   B
  What a gift here below

E♭   Em
  But no one knows.

          B
Gift that you give to me

E♭   Em
  No one knows.

Outro | Em | Em | Em   ‖

RADIOHEAD: Creep

Words & Music by
Thom Yorke, Jonny Greenwood, Colin Greenwood, Ed O'Brien, Phil Selway,
Albert Hammond & Mike Hazlewood

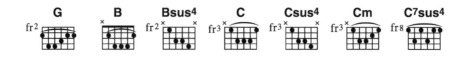

Intro | G | G | B | Bsus⁴ B |

| C | Csus⁴ C | Cm | Cm ||

Verse 1

                 G
When you were here before

                B
Couldn't look you in the eye,

         C
You're just like an angel,

           Cm
Your skin makes me cry.

        G
You float like a feather

        B
In a beautiful world.

     C
I wish I was special,

         Cm
You're so fuckin' special

Chorus 1

      G   **B**
But I'm a creep, I'm a weirdo.

             C
What the hell am I doing here?

    Cm   **C⁷sus⁴**
I don't be - long here.

Verse 2

            G
I don't care if it hurts,

       B
I wanna have control,

     C
I wanna perfect body,

cont.

       Cm
I wanna perfect soul.

    G
I want you to notice

      B
When I'm not around,

       C
You're so fuckin' special

      Cm
I wish I was special...

Chorus 2

      G   **B**
But I'm a creep, I'm a weirdo.

         C
What the hell am I doing here?

     Cm
I don't be - long here.

C⁷sus⁴
Oh, oh.

Bridge

 G   **B**
She's running out a - gain,

C
She's running out

   Cm
She's run, run, run,

G **B C** **Cm**
Run.   Run...

Verse 3

       G
Whatever makes you happy

    B
Whatever you want,

    C
You're so fuckin' special

    Cm
I wish I was special...

Chorus 3

      G   **B**
But I'm a creep, I'm a weirdo,

        C
What the hell am I doing here?

    Cm
I don't be - long here,

    G
I don't be - long here.

RAGE AGAINST THE MACHINE: Wake Up

Words by Zack De La Rocha
Music by Rage Against The Machine

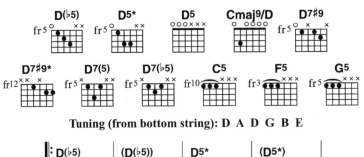

Tuning (from bottom string): D A D G B E

Intro

:‖ D(♭5)	(D(♭5))	D5*	(D5*)	
D(♭5)	(D(♭5))	D5*	(D5*)	‖:
D5	(D5)	Cmaj9/D	(Cmaj9/D)	
D5	(D5)	N.C.	N.C.	‖

Come on!

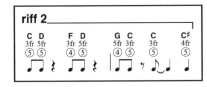

| (D5) | (D5) | (D5) | (D5) | | N.C. (D5*) :‖ |

riff 2

Verse 1

N.C.(D5)   w/riff 2
Come on, although ya try to dis - credit,   Ya still never read it

                          w/riff 2
The needle, I'll thread it, Radically poetic

                          w/riff 2
Standin' with the fury that they had in '66

                     w/riff 2
And like E-Double I'm mad, Still knee-deep in the system's shit

w/riff 2
Hoover, he was a body remover

           w/riff 2
I'll give ya a dose, But it can never come close

                     w/riff 2
To the rage built up inside of me

w/riff 2 N.C.
Fist in the air, in the land of hypocrisy.

Verse 2

w/riff 2
Movements come and movements go

w/riff 2
Leaders speak, movements cease

When their heads are flown

w/riff 2
'Cause all these punks got bullets in their heads

     D7♯9
De - partments of police, the judges, the feds.

w/riff 2
Networks at work, keepin' people calm

       w/riff 2
You know they went after King

When he spoke out on Vietnam

w/riff 2
He turned the power to the have-nots

w/riff 2 N.C.
And then came the shot.

Link 1

riff 1 _____ riff 1 _____

‖: (D5) | (D5) | (D5) | (D5) |

|1 |2.

riff 1 _____ riff 1

| (D5) | (D5) | (D5) | N.C. (D5*) :‖ D7♯9* | (D7♯9*) ‖

Verse 3

w/riff 2
Wit' poetry, my mind I flex

   w/riff 2
Flip like Wilson, vocals never lackin' dat finesse

w/riff 2
Whadda I got to, whadda I got to do to wake ya up

  w/riff 3
To shake ya up, to break the structure up

    w/riff 2
'Cause blood still flows in the gutter

      w/riff 2
I'm like takin' photos

Mad boy kicks open the shutter

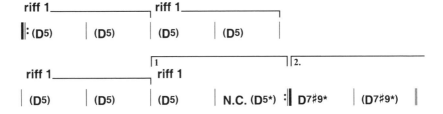

w/riff 2
Set the groove

Then stick and move like I was Cassius

w/riff 2 N.C.
Rep the stutter step, Then bomb a left upon the fascists.

Verse 4

w/riff 2 **w/riff 2**

Yea, the several federal men who pulled schemes on the dream

w/riff 2

And put it to an end Ya better beware

Of retribution with mind war

D7(5) **D7(♭5)**

20/20 visions and murals with metaphors

w/riff 2

Networks at work, keepin' people calm

w/riff 2

Ya know they murdered X

And tried to blame it on Islam

w/riff 2

He turned the power to the have-nots

w/riff 2 N.C.

And then came the shot.

Middle

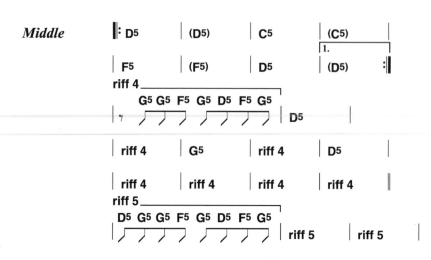

Bridge

w/riff 5 *(x4)*

What was the price on his head?

w/riff 5 **D5***

What was the price on his head!

(D5*)

I think I heard a shot

I think I heard a shot

I think I heard a shot

riff 6 _____

| D(♭5) | (D(♭5)) | D5* | (D5*) |

| D(♭5) | (D(♭5)) | D5* | (D5*) |

I think I heard a shot

w/riff 6
I think I heard a shot

I think I heard,

N.C.
I think I heard a shot.

| (D5) | (D5) | (D5) | (D5) |

Verse 5

D5   **Cmaj⁹/D**
'He may be a real contender for this position should he

      D5
abandon his supposed obedience to white liberal doctrine

     Cmaj⁹/D
of non-violence... and embrace black nationalism'

D5   **Cmaj⁹/D**
'Through counter-intelligence it should be possible to

          D5
pinpoint potential trouble-makers ... and neutralize them.

      Cmaj⁹/D
Through counter-intelligence it should be possible to

       D5
pinpoint potential trouble-makers ...   and neutralize them

    N.C.
and neutralize them, and neutralize them, and neutralize them.'

Outro

w/riff 1 *(x3)*   **D5**
Wake up! Wake up! Wake up! Wake up!

w/riff 1 *(x4)*   **w/riff 1** *(ad lib.)*
Wake up! Wake up! Wake up! Wake up!

N.C.(D5)   **N.C.**
How long? Not long, cause what you reap is what you sow

REM: Crazy

Words & Music by
Michael Lachowski, Curtis Crowe, Vanessa Briscoe & Randall Bewley

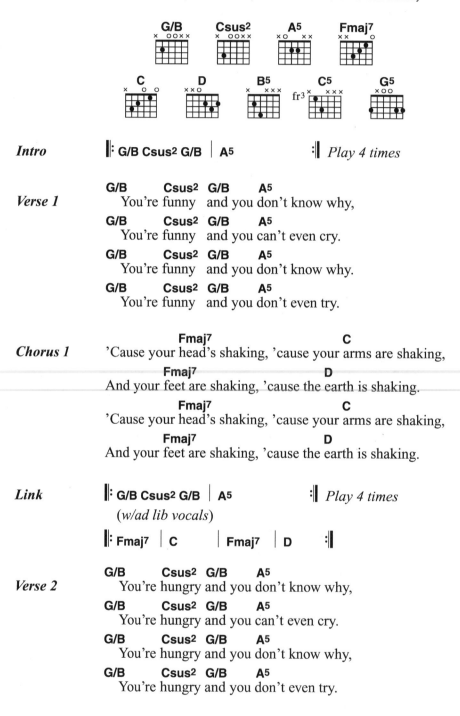

Intro

‖: G/B Csus2 G/B | A5 :‖ *Play 4 times*

Verse 1

G/B   Csus2 G/B   A5
You're funny and you don't know why,
G/B   Csus2 G/B   A5
You're funny and you can't even cry.
G/B   Csus2 G/B   A5
You're funny and you don't know why.
G/B   Csus2 G/B   A5
You're funny and you don't even try.

Chorus 1

         Fmaj7   C
'Cause your head's shaking, 'cause your arms are shaking,
       Fmaj7   D
And your feet are shaking, 'cause the earth is shaking.
         Fmaj7   C
'Cause your head's shaking, 'cause your arms are shaking,
       Fmaj7   D
And your feet are shaking, 'cause the earth is shaking.

Link

‖: G/B Csus2 G/B | A5 :‖ *Play 4 times*
(*w/ad lib vocals*)

‖: Fmaj7 | C | Fmaj7 | D :‖

Verse 2

G/B   Csus2 G/B   A5
You're hungry and you don't know why,
G/B   Csus2 G/B   A5
You're hungry and you can't even cry.
G/B   Csus2 G/B   A5
You're hungry and you don't know why,
G/B   Csus2 G/B   A5
You're hungry and you don't even try.

Chorus 2

       Fmaj7   **C**
'Cause your head's shaking, 'cause your arms are shaking,

          Fmaj7   **D**
And your feet are shaking, 'cause the earth is shaking.

          Fmaj7   **C**
And your head's shaking, and your arms are shaking,

          Fmaj7   **D**
And your feet are shaking, 'cause the earth is shaking.

Bridge

A5 **B5** **C5** **B5**   **A5**
You take a walk and you try to understand.

(E)   **G5**   **A5** **B5** **C5**   **B5** **A5**
Nothing can hurt you, un - less you want it   to.

(E)   **G5**   **A5** **B5** **C5**   **B5** **A5**
There are no ans - wers, ma - ny   reasons to be strong.

(E)   **G5**
You take a walk, you take a walk,

A5 **B5**   **C5** **B5**   **A5**   **(E)** **G5**
You take a walk and you try to understand, oh

Interlude

‖: **Fmaj7** | **C** | **Fmaj7** | **D**   :‖

‖: **G/B Csus2 G/B** | **A5**   :‖ *Play 4 times*

Chorus 3

       Fmaj7   **C**
'Cause your head's shaking, 'cause your arms are shaking,

          Fmaj7   **D**
And your feet are shaking, 'cause the earth is shaking.

          Fmaj7   **C**
And your head's shaking, And your arms are shaking,

          Fmaj7   **D**
And your feet are shaking, 'cause the earth is shaking.

Outro

G/B   **Csus2** **G/B**   **A5**
  You're in love   and you don't know why,

G/B   **Csus2** **G/B**   **A5**
  You're in love   and you can't even cry.

G/B   **Csus2** **G/B**   **A5**
  You're in love   and you don't know why,

G/B   **Csus2** **G/B**   **A5**
  You're in love   and you didn't even try.

JONATHAN RICHMAN & THE MODERN LOVERS:
Roadrunner

Words & Music by
Jonathan Richman

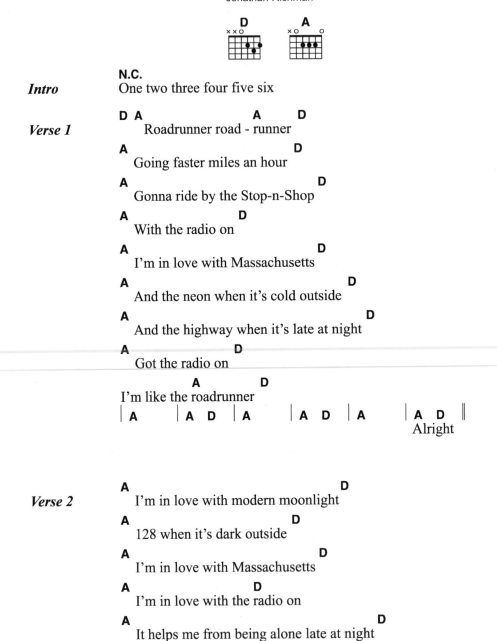

N.C.

Intro One two three four five six

Verse 1

D A   A   D
   Roadrunner road - runner

A   D
Going faster miles an hour

A   D
Gonna ride by the Stop-n-Shop

A   D
With the radio on

A   D
I'm in love with Massachusetts

A   D
And the neon when it's cold outside

A   D
And the highway when it's late at night

A   D
Got the radio on

          A   D
I'm like the roadrunner

| A | A D | A | A D | A | A D ‖
Alright

Verse 2

A   D
I'm in love with modern moonlight

A   D
128 when it's dark outside

A   D
I'm in love with Massachusetts

A   D
I'm in love with the radio on

A   D
It helps me from being alone late at night

A   D
It helps me from being lonely late at night

A   D
I don't feel so bad now in the car

       A
Like the Roadrunner

       D
That's right

| **A** | | **A** | **D** | **A** | | **A** | **D** | **A** | | **A** | **D** |‖

Verse 3

    A   **D**
Said welcome to the spirit of 1956

A   **D**
Patient in the bushes next to '57

       A   **D**
The highway is your girlfriend as you go by quick

             A
Suburban trees, suburban speed

       A   **D**
And it smells like heaven

            A
And I say roadrunner once

Roadrunner twice

N.C.   **A**
I'm in love with rock and roll and I'll be out all night

Roadrunner

       D
That's right

Instr.

‖:**A** | **A** **D** :‖ *Play 15 times*

| **A** | | **A** | **D** | **A** | | **A** | **D** |‖
                Well now

Verse 4

A   **D**
  Roadrunner, roadrunner

A   **D**
  Going faster miles an hour

A   **D**
  Gonna drive to the Stop 'n' Shop

A   **D**
  With the radio on at night

And me in love with modern moonlight

A   **D**
  Me in love with modern rock and roll

A   **D**
  Modern girls and modern rock and roll

A   **D**
  Don't feel so alone, got the radio on

       A
Like the roadrunner

O.K., now you sing Modern Lovers

D   A
(Radio On!)

I got the AM

D   A
(Radio On!)

Got the car, got the AM

D   A
(Radio On!)

Got the AM sound

D   A
(Radio On!)

Got the rockin' modern neon sound

D   A
(Radio On!)

I got the car from Massachusetts, got the

D   A
(Radio On!)

I got the power of Massachusetts when it's late at night

D   A
(Radio On!)

I got the modern sounds of modern Massachusetts

D   A
(Radio On!)

                                          D   A
I've got the world, got the turnpike, got the (Radio On)

I've got the, got the power of the AM

             D   A
Got the (Radio On)

                      D   A
Late at night, rock & roll (Radio On)

The factories and the auto signs got the power of modern sounds

Outro

A D	A	A D	A	
	Alright			

A D	A	A D	A D

A D	A D	A E	A	‖
	Right,	bye bye!		

ROXY MUSIC: Ladytron

Words & Music by
Bryan Ferry

Am   Em   G   D   E fr7   D fr5   B fr7   A fr5

Tune guitar down a semitone

Free time - ad lib.

Intro ‖: N.C. :‖

      Am   Em
You've got me girl on the run around, run around,
      G   D
You've got me all around town.
      Am   Em
You've got me girl on the run around
G   D   E
And it's getting me down, getting me down.

Verse 1
      E   D
Lady, if you want to find a lover,
             B
Then you look no further,
            A
For I'm gonna be your only.
      E   D
Searching at the start of the season,
           B   A
And my only reason, Is that I'll get to you.

Interlude ‖: E | E | D | D ‖
              | B | B | A | A :‖

Verse 2
      E   D
I'll find some way of connection,
           B
Hiding my in - tention,
           A
Then I'll move up close to you.
      E   D
I'll use you, and I'll con - fuse you,
           B   A
And the I'll lose you, Still you won't sus - pect me.

Solo ‖: E | E | D | D ‖
        | B | B | A | A :‖ *Repeat to fade*

THE SAINTS: This Perfect Day

Words & Music by
Ed Keupper & Chris Bailey

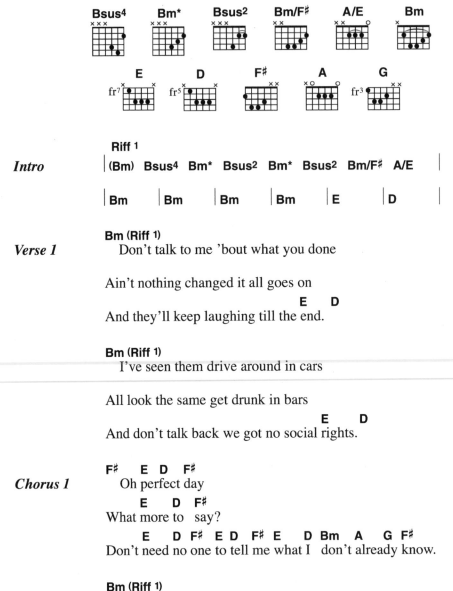

Riff 1

Intro

| (Bm) Bsus4 Bm* Bsus2 Bm* Bsus2 Bm/F♯ A/E |

| Bm | Bm | Bm | Bm | E | D |

Verse 1

Bm (Riff 1)
Don't talk to me 'bout what you done

Ain't nothing changed it all goes on

                                E   D
And they'll keep laughing till the end.

Bm (Riff 1)
I've seen them drive around in cars

All look the same get drunk in bars

                               E   D
And don't talk back we got no social rights.

Chorus 1

  F♯   E D F♯
Oh perfect day
      E   D F♯
What more to say?
        E   D F♯ E D F♯ E   D Bm A G F♯
Don't need no one to tell me what I don't already know.

Verse 2

Bm (Riff 1)
We got no high times always flat

If you go out you don't come back

                    E   D
It's all so funny I can't laugh.

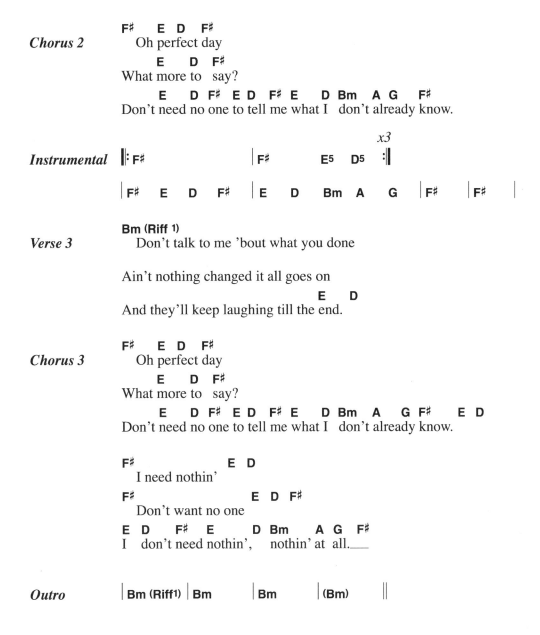

Chorus 2

    F♯   E D F♯
    Oh perfect day

        E   D F♯
What more to say?

          E   D F♯ E D F♯ E   D Bm A G   F♯
Don't need no one to tell me what I don't already know.

Instrumental

                                                      x3

‖: F♯ | F♯   E5   D5   :‖

| F♯ E D   F♯ | E   D   Bm A   G | F♯ | F♯ |

Verse 3

Bm (Riff 1)
    Don't talk to me 'bout what you done

Ain't nothing changed it all goes on

                         E   D
And they'll keep laughing till the end.

Chorus 3

    F♯   E D F♯
    Oh perfect day

        E   D F♯
What more to say?

          E   D F♯ E D F♯ E   D Bm A   G F♯   E D
Don't need no one to tell me what I don't already know.

    F♯   E D
    I need nothin'

    F♯   E D F♯
    Don't want no one

E D   F♯ E   D Bm   A G F♯
I   don't need nothin',   nothin' at all.__

Outro

| Bm (Riff1) | Bm | Bm | (Bm)   ‖

SEBADOH: The Freed Pig

Words & Music by
Lou Barlow

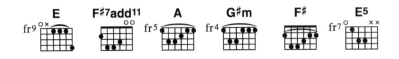

Intro   ‖: E | (C#bass) (B bass) | F#7add11 | F#7add11 :‖

Verse 1
         E
You were right,

I was battling you,
F#7add11
Trying to prove myself.
   E   **F#7add11**
  I tried to bury you with guilt,
                        E
I wanted to prove you wrong.
                        F#7add11
I've got nothing better to do,
                        E
Than pay too much attention to you.
                   F#7add11
It's sad, but it's not your fault.

Chorus 1
      A   **G#m**
Self-righteous and rude,
   A   **G#m**
I guess I lost that cool,
   A   **G#m**   **F#**
Tapping 'til I drive you in - sane.
   A   **G#m**
I'm self-righteous, but never right,
   A   **G#m**
So laid back, but so uptight.
         A   **G#m**
Des - troying your patience to tolerate me,
   F#7add11
With all the negative spirit I bring.

Link | E | (C#bass) (B bass) | F#7add11 | F#7add11 |

Verse 2

E   F#7add11
Right, I was obsessed to bring you down,

                     E
Watching your every move.

                F#7add11
Playing a little boy game,

                     E
Always with something to prove.

                F#7add11
Waiting to cut you down,

              E
Making it hard to live.

                   F#7add11
With only one thing to do,

Cut me first, make it easy.

Chorus 2

A   G#m
  Now you will be free,

 A   G#m
  Now that nothing de - pends on me,

A   G#m   F#7
Tapping 'til I drive you in - sane.

A   G#m
  Now you will be free,

    A   G#m
With no sick people tugging on your sleeve.

    A   G#m   F#7add11
Your big head has that more room to grow,

A glory I will never know,

A glory I will never know.

Solo   ‖: E5 | E5 | F#7add11 | F#7add11 :‖ *Repeat to fade*

SIGUR RÓS: Hoppípolla

Words & Music by
Jon Birgisson, Orri Dryasson, Georg Holm & Kjartan Sveinsson

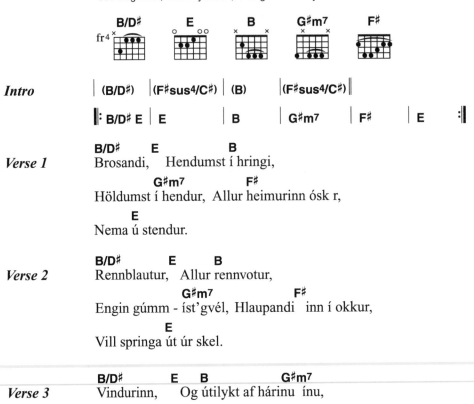

Intro
| (B/D#) | (F#sus4/C#) | (B) | (F#sus4/C#) |

‖: B/D# E | E | B | G#m7 | F# | E :‖

Verse 1

B/D#   E   B
Brosandi,   Hendumst í hringi,

       G#m7   F#
Höldumst í hendur, Allur heimurinn ósk r,

       E
Nema ú stendur.

Verse 2

B/D#   E   B
Rennblautur,   Allur rennvotur,

       G#m7   F#
Engin gúmm - íst'gvél, Hlaupandi   inn í okkur,

       E
Vill springa út úr skel.

Verse 3

B/D#   E   B   G#m7
Vindurinn,   Og útilykt af hárinu ínu,

       F#   E
Eg lamdi eins fast og ég get, Me nefinu mínu.

Bridge

B   F#   E
Hoppí - polla, I engum stígvélum,

B/D#   B   F#   E   F#
    Allur rennvotur, rennblautur,   I engum stígvélum.

Chorus 1

       B/D#   E
Og ég fæ blónasir,

       B/D# E
En ég stend alltaf upp,

Hopelandic.

‖: B | G#m7 | F# | E :‖

Chorus 2   As Chorus 1

Outro   ‖: B | G#m7 | F# | E :‖ *Play 4 times*

| B |

SONIC YOUTH: Sugar Kane

Words & Music by
Kim Gordon, Thurston Moore, Lee Ranaldo & Steve Shelley

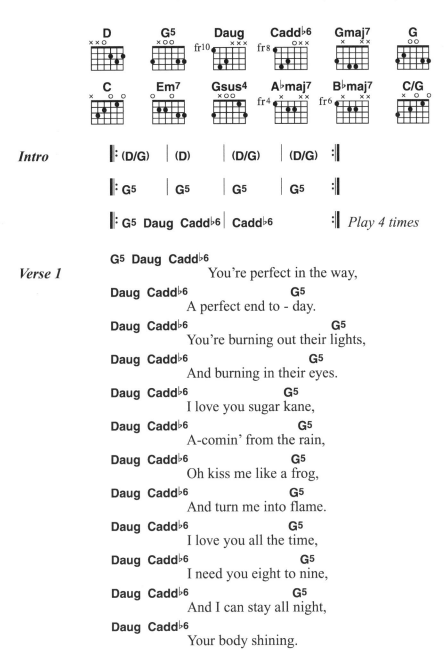

Intro

$\parallel$: (D/G) | (D) | (D/G) | (D/G) :$\parallel$

$\parallel$: G5 | G5 | G5 | G5 :$\parallel$

$\parallel$: G5 Daug Cadd$\flat$6 | Cadd$\flat$6 :$\parallel$ *Play 4 times*

Verse 1

G5 Daug Cadd$\flat$6
    You're perfect in the way,
Daug Cadd$\flat$6   G5
    A perfect end to - day.
Daug Cadd$\flat$6   G5
    You're burning out their lights,
Daug Cadd$\flat$6   G5
    And burning in their eyes.
Daug Cadd$\flat$6   G5
    I love you sugar kane,
Daug Cadd$\flat$6   G5
    A-comin' from the rain,
Daug Cadd$\flat$6   G5
    Oh kiss me like a frog,
Daug Cadd$\flat$6   G5
    And turn me into flame.
Daug Cadd$\flat$6   G5
    I love you all the time,
Daug Cadd$\flat$6   G5
    I need you eight to nine,
Daug Cadd$\flat$6   G5
    And I can stay all night,
Daug Cadd$\flat$6
    Your body shining.

Chorus 1

Gmaj7   **Cadd♭6**
    And I know,

                Gmaj7   **Cadd♭6**
There's something down there, sugar soul.

          Gmaj7   **Cadd♭6**
Back to the cross, a twisted lane,

              Gmaj7   **Cadd♭6**
There something down there sugar kane.

Link 1 | **Cadd♭6** | **Cadd♭6** | **N.C.** | **N.C.** | **G5** | **G5** ‖

Verse 2

G5 **Daug** **Cadd♭6**   **G5**
    I'm back again in love,

Daug **Cadd♭6**   **G5**
    I'm back again a dove.

Daug **Cadd♭6**   **G5**
    Where'd you get your light?

Daug **Cadd♭6**   **G5**
    Your smilin' sugar life.

Daug **Cadd♭6**   **G5**
    Another lovers day,

Daug **Cadd♭6**   **G5**
    Another cracked up night,

Daug **Cadd♭6**   **G5**
    Every night I say,

Daug **Cadd♭6**
    The light is coming.

Chorus 2

Gmaj7   **Cadd♭6**
    And I know,

                Gmaj7   **Cadd♭6**
There's something down there, sugar soul.

          Gmaj7   **Cadd♭6**
Back to the cross, a twisted lane,

              Gmaj7   **Cadd♭6**
There something down there sugar kane.

Link 2 | Cadd♭6 | Cadd♭6 | N.C. | N.C. |

| G5 | G5 | G5 | G5 ‖

Solo   ‖: (D/G) | (D) | (D/G) | (D/G) :‖

‖: (G) | (G) | (C) | (C) :‖ *Play 7 times*

‖: Em7 | Em7 | Em7 | Em7 :‖ *Play 3 times*

‖: G | Gsus4 | G | Gsus4 :‖

‖: Gmaj7 | A♭maj7 B♭maj7 :‖ *Play 10 times*

| G5 | G5 | G5 | G5 |

| G | C/G | G | C/G ‖

Verse 3

G5 Daug Cadd♭6   G5
                    Hey angel come and play,
Daug Cadd♭6   G5
          And fly me a - way.
Daug Cadd♭6   G5
          A stroll along the beach,
Daug Cadd♭6   G5
          Until you're out of time.
Daug Cadd♭6   G5
          I love you sugar kane,
Daug Cadd♭6   G5
          A crack into the dream.
‖: Daug Cadd♭6   G5
          I love you sugar kane :‖ *Play 5 times*
Daug Cadd♭6   G5
          I love you sugar.

SIOUSXIE & THE BANSHEES: Spellbound

Words & Music by
Steve Severin, Susan Ballion, Peter Clarke & John McGeoch

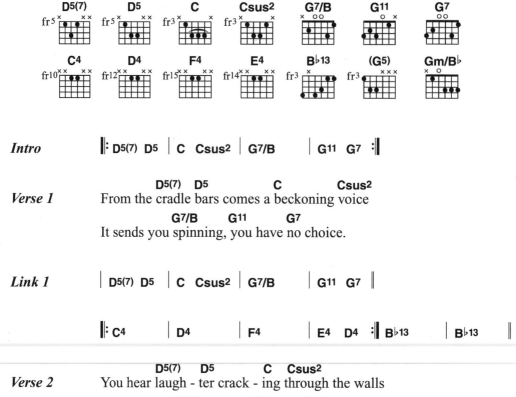

Intro
‖: D5(7) D5 | C Csus2 | G7/B | G11 G7 :‖

Verse 1

                D5(7)   D5   C   Csus2
From the cradle bars comes a beckoning voice

              G7/B   G11   G7
It sends you spinning, you have no choice.

Link 1
| D5(7) D5 | C Csus2 | G7/B | G11 G7 ‖

‖: C4 | D4 | F4 | E4 D4 :‖ B♭13 | B♭13 ‖

Verse 2

                D5(7)   D5   C Csus2
You hear laugh - ter crack - ing through the walls

              G7/B   G11   G7
It sends you spinning, you have no choice.

                D5(7)   D5   C   Csus2
You hear laugh - ter crack - ing through the walls

              G7/B   G11 G7
It sends you spinning, you have no choice.

Chorus 1

C4   D4
Following the footsteps of a rag doll dance

     F4   E4   D4
We are entranced, spellbound

C4   D4
Following the footsteps of a rag doll dance

     F4   E4   D4 C4   D4   F4 | E4 D4 |
We are entranced, spellbound, spellbound, spellbound oh.

C4   D4   F4   E4   D4 B♭13 | B♭13 | B♭13 | B♭13 ‖
Spellbound, spellbound, spellbound, spell - bound.

Verse 3

    D5(7) D5   **C Csus2**   **G7/B**
And don't forget when your el - ders forget

       G11 G7   **D5(7) D5** **C Csus2**   **G7/B**
To say their pray - ers, take   them by the legs

     G11   G7
And throw them down the stairs.

Link 2

| **D5(7) D5** | **C Csus2** | **G7/B** | **C Csus2** |

| **D5(7) D5** | **C Csus2** | **G7/B** | **Gm/B♭**   ‖

Verse 4

           D5(7) D5   **C   Csus2**
When do you think your toys have gone ber - serk

        G7/B   **G11**   **G7**
It's an illusion, you can - not shirk

         D5(7)   **D5 C**   **Csus2**
You hear laugh - ter crack - ing through the walls

            G7/B   **G11**   **G7**
It sends you spinning you have no choice.

Chorus 2

C4   **D4**
Following the footsteps of a rag doll dance

     F4   **E4**   **D4**
We are entranced, spellbound

C4   **D4**
Following the footsteps of a rag doll dance

     F4   **E4**   **D4**   **C4**   **D4**   **E4**   **D4**
We are entranced, spell - bound, spellbound, spellbound, oh spell - bound

C4   **D4**   **F4**   **E4**   **D4**
Spellbound, spellbound, spellbound, spell - bound.

Link 3

‖: **C4** | **D4** | **F4** | **E4 D4** :‖ **C4** | **D4** | **F4** ‖

Chorus 3

      E4   **D4**   **C4**   **D4**
Follow - ing the footsteps of a rag doll dance

      F4
We are entranced,

      E4   **D4**   **C4**   **D4**
Follow - ing the footsteps of a rag doll dance

      F4
We are entranced, entranced, entranced

E4   **D4**
Dance, dance, dance.

| **C4** | **D4** | **(G5)** ‖

THE SISTERS OF MERCY: Temple Of Love

Words & Music by
Craig Adams & Andrew Eldritch

E5   G5   A5   B5   C5   G5/D

Intro ‖: E5 | G5 | A5 | (B) (C) (D) :‖ *Play 4 times*

Verse 1

E5   G5   A5
With the fire from the fireworks up a - round me,
        E5   G5   A5
With a gun for a lover and a shot for the pain at hand.
        E5   G5
You run for cover in the Temple of Love,
        A5
You run for another but still the same,
        E5   G5   A5
For the wind will blow my name across this land.
E5   G5   A5
  In the temple of love you hide to - gether,
E5   G5   A5
  Believing pain and fear out - side.
        E5   G5
But someone near you rides the weather,
A5   E5
And the tears he cried will rain on walls,
            G5   A5
As wide as   lovers eyes.

Chorus 1

            E5   A5 B5 C5
In the Temple of Love,
G5   A5   B5
Shine like thun - der.
E5   A5 B5 C5
  In the Temple of Love,
G5   A5   B5
Cry like rain.
E5   A5 B5 C5
  In the Temple of Love,

G5   A5   B5
Hear my call - ing.
E5   A5 B5 C5
  In the Temple of Love,
G5   A5   B5
Hear my name.

Verse 2

  E5   G5   A5
And the devil in a black dress watches over,

  E5   G5   A5
My guardian angel walks a - way.

  E5   G5   A5
Life is short and love is always over in the morning,

  E5   G5   A5
Black wind come carry me far a - way.

  E5   G5   A5
With the sunlight died and the night a - bove me,

     E5   G5   A5
With a gun for a lover and a shot for the pain in - side.

     E5   G5
You run for cover in the Temple of Love,

     A5
You run for another it's all the same,

     E5   G5   A5
For the wind will blow and throw your walls a - side.

Chorus 2

     E5
With the fire from the fireworks up above,

    A5   B5   C5 G5   A5
With a gun for a lover and a shot for the pain.

B5 E5
You run for cover in the Temple of Love,

A5   B5   C5 G5   A5
Shine like thun - der cry like rain.

B5   E5
And the Temple of Love grows old and strong,

    A5   B5   C5 G5   A5
But the wind blows strong - er   cold and long.

B5   E5
And the Temple of Love will fall before,

    A5   B5 C5 G5   A5 B5
This black wind calls my name to you no more.

Link   ‖: E5   │ G5   │ A5   │ (B) (C) (D) :‖ *Play 4 times*

Verse 3

     E5   G5
In the black sky thunder sweeping,

     A5
Under - ground and over water,

       E5   G5
Sounds of crying, weeping will not save,

    A5
Your faith for bricks and dreams for mortar.

E5   G5
All your prayers must seem as nothing,

A5
Ninety-six below the wave,

    E5   G5
When stone is dust and only air re - mains.

Chorus 3

E5   A5 B5 C5
In the Temple of Love,

G5   A5   B5
Shine like thun - der.

E5   A5 B5 C5
  In the Temple of Love,

G5   A5   B5
Cry like rain.

E5   A5 B5 C5
  In the Temple of Love,

G5   A5   B5
Hear the call - ing.

E5   A5 B5 C5
  In the Temple of Love,

G5 A5   B5 E5
Is   fall - ing down.

Interlude

‖: N.C.   :‖ *17 bars*

‖: E5 | G5/D | A5 | A5   :‖ *Play 8 times*

Chorus 4

E5   A5 B5 C5
In the Temple of Love,

G5   A5   B5
Shine like thun - der.

E5   A5 B5 C5
  In the Temple of Love,

G5   A5   B5
Cry like rain.

E5   A5 B5 C5
  In the Temple of Love,

G5   A5   B5
Hear my call - ing.

E5   A5 B5 C5
  In the Temple of Love,

G5   A5 E5
Hear my name.

Verse 4

       E5   G5/D
In the black sky thunder sweeping,

        A5
Under - ground and over water,

          E5   G5/D
Sounds of crying, weeping will not save,

       A5
Your faith for bricks and dreams for mortar.

E5   G5/D
All your prayers must seem as nothing,

A5
Ninety-six below the wave,

E5   **G5/D**
When stone is dust and air remains.

    A5
The only haven you can trust.

      E5   **G5/D**   **A5**
And the devil in a black dress watches over,

E5   **G5/D**   **A5**
  My guardian angel walks a - way.

E5   **G5/D**   **A5**
  Life is short and love is always over in the morning,

E5   **G5/D**   **A5**
  Black wind come carry me far a - way.

             E5
Chorus 5   With the fire from the fireworks up above,

      A5   **B5** **C5** **G5**   **A5**
With a gun for a lover and a shot for the pain.

B5 **E5**
You run for cover in the Temple of Love,

A5   **B5**   **C5** **G5**   **A5**
Shine like thun - der cry like rain.

B5   **E5**
And the Temple of Love grows old and strong,

      A5   **B5**   **C5** **G5**   **A5**
But the wind blows strong - er   cold and long.

B5   **E5**
And the Temple of Love will fall before,

      A5   **B5** **C5** **G5**   **A5** **B5**
This black wind calls my name to you no more.

Link   ‖: **E5** | **G5** | **A5** | **A5** :‖ *Play 3 times*

        | **E5** | **G5** | **A5** | **(B) (C) (D)** ‖

E5   **G5**   **A5**
Verse 5   In the temple of love you hide to - gether,

E5   **G5**   **A5**
  Believing pain and fear out - side.

    E5   **G5**
But someone near you rides the weather,

A5   **E5**
And the tears he cried will rain on walls,

      G5   **A5**
As wide as   lovers eyes.

Chorus 6   As Chorus 3

SLINT: Good Morning, Captain

Words & Music by
Brian McMahan, Ethan Buckler, Britt Walford & David Pajo

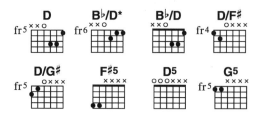

Tuning (from bottom string): D A D G B E

Intro ‖: D | Bb/D* | D | Bb/D* :‖ *Play 3 times*

Verse 1
(D)
"Let me in", the voice cried softly.
From outside the wooden door.
Scattered remnants of the ship, could be seen in the distance.
Blood stained the icy wall of the shore.

Link 1 ‖: D | Bb/D | D | Bb/D :‖

Verse 2
(D)
"I'm the only one left, the storm, took them all."
He managed as he tried to stand.
The tears ran down his face.
"Please, it's cold."

Solo 1 | D | Bb/D | D | Bb/D |

‖: (D) | (D) | D/F# | D/G# :‖

| (D) | (D) | (D) | (D) ‖

Verse 3
(D)
When he woke, there was no trace of the ship.
Only the dawn was left behind by the storm.
He felt the creaking of the stairs beneath him.
That rose, from the sea, to the door.

Link 2 ‖: D | Bb/D | D | Bb/D :‖

Verse 4
(D)
There was a sound at the window then.
The captain started, his breath was still.
Slowly, he turned.

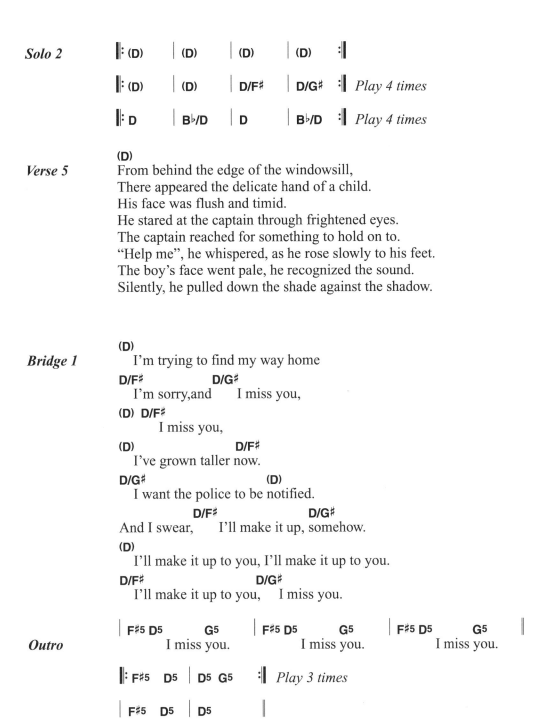

Solo 2 ‖: (D) | (D) | (D) | (D) :‖

‖: (D) | (D) | D/F♯ | D/G♯ :‖ *Play 4 times*

‖: D | B♭/D | D | B♭/D :‖ *Play 4 times*

Verse 5

(D)
From behind the edge of the windowsill,
There appeared the delicate hand of a child.
His face was flush and timid.
He stared at the captain through frightened eyes.
The captain reached for something to hold on to.
"Help me", he whispered, as he rose slowly to his feet.
The boy's face went pale, he recognized the sound.
Silently, he pulled down the shade against the shadow.

Bridge 1

(D)
I'm trying to find my way home
D/F♯   D/G♯
I'm sorry,and   I miss you,
(D) D/F♯
I miss you,
(D)   D/F♯
I've grown taller now.
D/G♯   (D)
I want the police to be notified.
          D/F♯   D/G♯
And I swear,   I'll make it up, somehow.
(D)
I'll make it up to you, I'll make it up to you.
D/F♯   D/G♯
I'll make it up to you,   I miss you.

Outro

| F♯5 D5   G5 | F♯5 D5   G5 | F♯5 D5   G5 ‖
          I miss you.   I miss you.   I miss you.

‖: F♯5   D5 | D5 G5 :‖ *Play 3 times*

| F♯5   D5 | D5   ‖

153

PATTI SMITH: Gloria

Words & Music by
Van Morrison

E   D   A   G

Intro　　|　E　D　|　E　D　|　E　D　|　E　D　‖

Verse 1

E   D   E   D   E   D E D
Jesus died for somebody's sins but not mine.

E   D   E   D E   D   E   D
Meltin' in a pot of thieves,　wild card　up my sleeve.

E   D   E   D   E
Thick　heart of stone, my sins my own,

            D   E
They be - long to me, me.

Verse 2

E   D   E   D E
People say be - ware!

      D   E   D E
But I don't care.

            D   E   D   E
The words are just rules and regu - lations to me, me.

Verse 3

E D   E   D E
I, I walk in a room,

         D   E   D E
You know I look so proud.

         D   E   D   E
I'm movin' in this here atmosphere,　well,

D   E   D E
Anything's al - lowed.

         D   E   D
And I go to this here party

    E D   E   D
And I　just get bored.

      E   D   E   D
Until I look out the window, see a sweet young thing,

E   D   E   D
Humpin' on the parking meter, leanin' on the parking meter.

E   D   E   D
Oh, she looks so good,

E   D   E   D
Oh, she looks so fine.

      E   D E   D   E   D
And I got this crazy feeling and then I'm gonna ah-ah, make her mine.

```
E       D       E               D
Ooh I'll put my spell on her.


                (D)        E       D
Verse 4         Here she comes,
                        E                       D
                Walkin' down the street.
                        E       D
                Here she comes,
                        E                       D
                Comin' through my door.
                        E       D
                Here she comes,
                        E               D
                Crawlin' up my stair.
                        E       D
                Here she comes,
                        E               D
                Waltzin' through the hall
                  E               D
                In a pretty red dress.
                        E       D       E       D
                And oh, she looks so good,
                E       D       E   D
                Oh, she looks so fine.
                        E           D   E   D           E       D
                And I got this crazy feeling that I'm gonna ah-ah, make her mine.

                E               D       E               D       E D
Verse 5         And then I hear this knockin' on my door,
                            E                   D       E D
                Hear this knockin' on my door.
                    E                   E           D
                And I look up into the big tower clock,
                            E       D           E           D
                And say, oh my God here's midnight!
                            E   D           E               D
                And my baby    is walkin' through the door,
                            E           D       E           D           E               D
                Leanin' on my couch she whispers to me and I take the big plunge.
                  E   D           E       D
                And oh, she was so good
                  E   D               E   D
                And oh, she was so fine.
                    E               D       E   D           E       D
                And I'm gonna tell the world that I just ah-ah, made her mine.


                    E       D       E                   D
Verse 6         And I said darling, tell me your name,
                    E               D
                She told me her name.
```

```
       E              D
She whispered to me,
       E                  D
She told me her name.
            E         D
And her name is,
            E         D
And her name is,
            E         D
And her name is,
            E         D
And her name is
E  D  A  D  E                                G
G. L. O. R. I, I, I, I, I, I, I, I, G-l-o-r-i-a
```

Chorus 1
```
       E      D       A
Gloria,   G-l-o-r-i-a.
       E      D       A
Gloria,   G-l-o-r-i-a.
       E      D       A
Gloria,   G-l-o-r-i-a.
       E      D       A
Gloria.
```

Link 1
```
‖ E        | D   A  | E        | D   A   ‖
```

Verse 7
```
E                         D   A
I was at the stadium.
              E                          D          A
There were twenty thousand girls calling their name out to me.
          E              D           A
Ma - rie and Ruth but to tell you the truth,
E                   D      A
I didn't hear them, I didn't see.
     E                  D          A
I let my eyes rise to the big tower clock,
         E                    D    A
And I heard those bells chimin' in my heart.
              E                    D          A
Going ding dong, ding dong, ding dong, ding dong.
E                      D          A
Ding dong, ding dong, ding dong, ding dong.
E                  D  A
Counting the time.
```

Instr.

‖: F♯5   F♯5/7 | F♯5   F♯5/7 | F♯5   F♯5/7 | A5   B5 |

| F♯5   F♯5/7 | F♯5   F♯5/7 | F♯5   F♯5/7 | A5   B5   :‖

Bridge

B5   D5   A
   There's a club, if you'd like to go,
     Esus4   C♯5   E5   F♯5
You could meet somebody who really loves you,
     Bsus2
So you go, and you stand on your own,
A   Esus4
   And you leave on your own,
      C♯5   E5   F♯riff
And you go home, and you cry and you want to die.

Instr.

‖: F♯5   F♯5/7 | F♯5   F♯5/7 | F♯5   F♯5/7 | A5   B5 |

| F♯5   F♯5/7 | F♯5   F♯5/7 | F♯5   F♯5/7 | A5   B5   :‖

Chorus 3

B5   D5   A   Esus4
  When you say it's gonna happen now,
C♯5   E5   F♯5*
  Well, when exactly do you mean?
     Bsus2   A   Esus4
See, I've already waited too long,
C♯5   E5   F♯riff
  And all my hope is gone.

Instr.

‖: F♯5   F♯5/7 | F♯5   F♯5/7 | F♯5   F♯5/7 | A5   B5 |

| F♯5   F♯5/7 | F♯5   F♯5/7 | F♯5   F♯5/7 | A5   B5   :‖

| B5   D5 | A   Esus4 | C♯5   E5 | F♯5* |

| B5   D5 | A   Esus4 | C♯5   E5 | F♯5   F♯5/7 |

‖: F♯5   F♯5/7 | F♯5   F♯5/7 | F♯5   F♯5/7 | A5   B5 |

| F♯5   F♯5/7 | F♯5   F♯5/7 | F♯5   F♯5/7 | A5   B5   :‖

Chorus 4   As Chorus 1

Coda

‖: F♯5   F♯5/7 | F♯5   F♯5/7 | F♯5   F♯5/7 | A5   B5 |

| F♯5   F♯5/7 | F♯5   F♯5/7 | F♯5   F♯5/7 | A5   B5   :‖

Fade

159

SMOG: Cold Blooded Old Times

Words & Music by
William Callahan

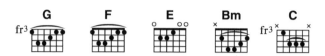

Tune guitar down a semitone

Intro | G | G | G | G   ‖

Chorus 1
    G
Cold-blooded old times.
        F
Cold-blooded old times.
        E   **F**
Cold-blooded old times.

Verse 1
    G
   The type of memories,
        F
That turns your bones to glass,
      E   **F**
Turns your bones to glass.
    G   **Bm**
   Mother came rushing in,
      C
She said we didn't see a thing,
      G
We said we didn't see a thing.
   Bm
And father left at eight,
     C
Nearly splintering the gate,
     G
Cold-blooded old times.

Chorus 2
Cold-blooded old times.
       F
Cold-blooded old times.
       E   **F**
Cold-blooded old times.

Verse 2

    G
    The type of memory,
              F
That turns your bones to glass,
           E   F
Turns your bones to glass.
G
And though you were,
    Bm
Just a little squirrel,
      C   G
You understood every word.
Bm
  And in this way,
         C
They gave you clarity,
         G
A cold-blooded clarity.

Chorus 3   Cold-blooded old times.
               F
Cold-blooded old times.
             E   F
Cold-blooded old times.

Bridge   ‖: G
         Now how can I stand,
        Bm
And laugh with the man,
C   G
  Who redefined your body. :‖

Chorus 4   Those Cold-blooded old times.
              F
Cold-blooded old times.
             E
Cold-blooded old times.

Solo   ‖: G | G | G | G   :‖ *Repeat ad lib. to end*

SOUNDGARDEN: Jesus Christ Pose

Words & Music by
Chris Cornell, Ben Shepherd, Matt Cameron & Kim Thayil

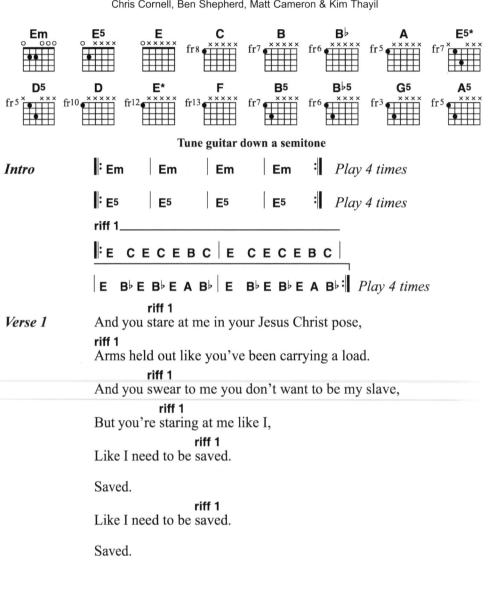

Tune guitar down a semitone

Intro	‖: Em	Em	Em	Em :‖ *Play 4 times*
	‖: E5	E5	E5	E5 :‖ *Play 4 times*

riff 1_____

‖: E C E C E B C | E C E C E B C |

| E B♭ E B♭ E A B♭ | E B♭ E B♭ E A B♭ :‖ *Play 4 times*

Verse 1

      riff 1
And you stare at me in your Jesus Christ pose,

riff 1
Arms held out like you've been carrying a load.

      riff 1
And you swear to me you don't want to be my slave,

      riff 1
But you're staring at me like I,

        riff 1
Like I need to be saved.

Saved.

        riff 1
Like I need to be saved.

Saved.

Chorus 1

      riff 1
In your Jesus Christ pose.

      riff 1
In your Jesus Christ pose.

Link   ‖: riff 1   :‖

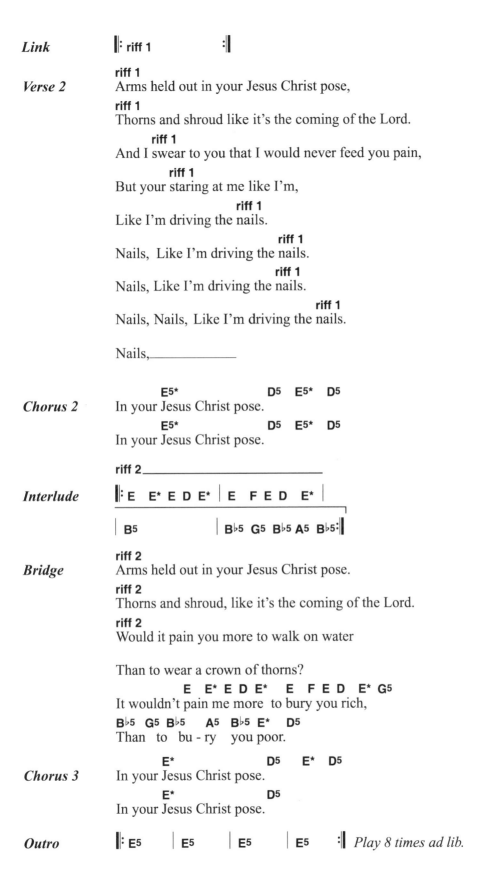

Link   ‖: riff 1   :‖

Verse 2
riff 1
Arms held out in your Jesus Christ pose,
riff 1
Thorns and shroud like it's the coming of the Lord.
    riff 1
And I swear to you that I would never feed you pain,
      riff 1
But your staring at me like I'm,
        riff 1
Like I'm driving the nails.
          riff 1
Nails, Like I'm driving the nails.
          riff 1
Nails, Like I'm driving the nails.
            riff 1
Nails, Nails, Like I'm driving the nails.

Nails,_____

Chorus 2
    E5*   D5 E5* D5
In your Jesus Christ pose.
    E5*   D5 E5* D5
In your Jesus Christ pose.

riff 2_____

Interlude   ‖: E   E* E D E* | E   F E D   E* |
  | B5 | B♭5 G5 B♭5 A5 B♭5:‖

Bridge
riff 2
Arms held out in your Jesus Christ pose.
riff 2
Thorns and shroud, like it's the coming of the Lord.
riff 2
Would it pain you more to walk on water

Than to wear a crown of thorns?
          E E* E D E*   E F E D E* G5
It wouldn't pain me more to bury you rich,
B♭5 G5 B♭5   A5 B♭5 E*   D5
Than to bu - ry   you poor.

Chorus 3
      E*   D5 E* D5
In your Jesus Christ pose.
      E*   D5
In your Jesus Christ pose.

Outro   ‖: E5 | E5 | E5 | E5   :‖ *Play 8 times ad lib.*

163

SPIRITUALIZED: Electricity

Words & Music by
Jason Pierce

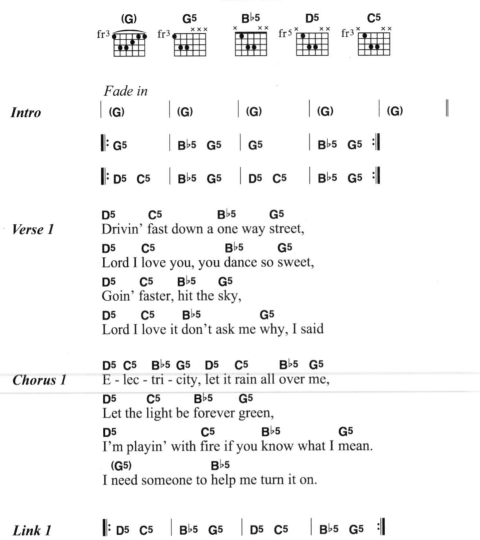

Fade in

Intro | (G) | (G) | (G) | (G) | (G)   ‖

‖: G5 | B♭5 G5 | G5 | B♭5 G5 :‖

‖: D5 C5 | B♭5 G5 | D5 C5 | B♭5 G5 :‖

Verse 1
D5   C5   B♭5   G5
Drivin' fast down a one way street,
D5   C5   B♭5   G5
Lord I love you, you dance so sweet,
D5   C5   B♭5   G5
Goin' faster, hit the sky,
D5   C5   B♭5   G5
Lord I love it don't ask me why, I said

Chorus 1
D5 C5 B♭5 G5 D5 C5   B♭5 G5
E - lec - tri - city, let it rain all over me,
D5   C5   B♭5   G5
Let the light be forever green,
D5   C5   B♭5   G5
I'm playin' with fire if you know what I mean.
 (G5)   B♭5
I need someone to help me turn it on.

Link 1   ‖: D5 C5 | B♭5 G5 | D5 C5 | B♭5 G5 :‖

Verse 2

D5   **C5**   **B♭5**   **G5**
Drivin' fast babe I'm on my own

D5   **C5**   **B♭5**   **G5**
I'm gonna meet you on a one way road

D5 **C5** **B♭5** **G5**
Gonna crash, kiss the sky

D5   **C5**   **B♭5**   **G5**
Lord I love you don't ask me why I said,

Chorus 2

D5 C5 **B♭5 G5** **D5**   **C5**   **B♭5 G5**
E - lec - tri - city, let it wash all over me,

D5   **C5**   **B♭5**   **G5**
Let the light be forever green,

     D5   **C5**   **B♭5**   **G5**
I'm playin' with fire if you know what I mean

 (G5)   **B♭5**
I need someone to help me turn it on.

Link 2

‖: **D5** **C5** | **B♭5** **G5** | **D5** **C5** | **B♭5** **G5** :‖

Verse 3

D5   **C5**   **B♭5**   **G5**
Drivin' fast down a one way street,

D5   **C5**   **B♭5**   **G5**
Lord I love you, you dance so neat,

D5 **C5**   **B♭5**   **G5**
Baby touch me, hit the sky,

D5 **C5**   **B♭5**   **G5**
Baby touch me, make me fly, I said

Chorus 3

D5 C5 **B♭5 G5**
E - lec - tri - city,

D5 C5 **B♭5 G5**
E - lec - tri - city,

D5 C5 **B♭5 G5**
E - lec - tri - city,

D5 C5 **B♭5 G5**
E - lec - tri - city, turn it on.

Outro

‖: **D5** **C5** | **B♭5** **G5** | **D5** **C5** | **B♭5** **G5** :‖ *Play 16 times*
w/ad lib. gtr.

STEREOLAB: French Disko

Words & Music by
Tim Gane & Laetitia Sadier

C5   Bb9sus4   Ab   Cm   Bb5/C   Ab5

Intro   ‖: C5 | C5 | C5 | C5 :‖

Verse 1

C5
Though this world's essentially,
   Bb9sus4
An absurd place to be living in,
   Ab   Cm
It doesn't call for bubble withdraw - al.
C5
I've been told it's a fact of life,
   Bb9sus4
Men have to kill one another,
   Ab   Cm
Well I say there are still things worth fighting for.
Bb5/C   C5
La resis - tance.

Verse 2

Though this world's essentially,
   Bb9sus4
An absurd place to be living in,
   Ab   Cm
It doesn't call for bubble withdraw - al.
C5
It said human existence is pointless,
   Bb9sus4   Ab
As acts of rebellious soli - darity,
                    Cm
Can bring sense in this world.
Bb5/C   C5   Bb5/C   C5
La resis - tance, La resis - tance.

Solo | C5 | C5 | Bb9sus4 | Bb9sus4 |

          | Ab | Ab | Cm | Cm |

cont.

C5	C5	B♭9sus4	B♭9sus4
A♭	A♭	Cm	Cm B♭5/C C5
C5	C5 B♭5/C C5	C5	C5 B♭5/C C5
C5	C5 B♭5/C C5		

Verse 3

C5
Though this world's essentially,

   B♭9sus4
An absurd place to be living in,

 A♭   Cm
It doesn't call for bubble withdraw - al.

C5
I've been told it's a fact of life,

   B♭9sus4
Men have to kill one another,

   A♭   Cm
Well I say there are still things worth fighting for.

B♭5/C   C5
La resis - tance.

Verse 4

Though this world's essentially,

   B♭9sus4
An absurd place to be living in,

 A♭   Cm
It doesn't call for bubble withdraw - al.

C5
It said human existence is pointless,

   B♭9sus4   A♭
As acts of rebellious soli - darity,

                  Cm
Can bring sense in this world.

B♭5/C   C5   B♭5/C   C5   B♭5/C C5
La resis - tance, La resis - tance,

Outro

C5	C5	B♭9sus4	B♭9sus4
A♭	A♭	Cm	Cm
C5	C5	B♭9sus4	B♭9sus4
A♭	A♭	Cm	Cm B♭5/C C5
‖: C5	C5 B♭5/C C5 :‖	*Repeat to fade*	

THE SUGARCUBES: Birthday

Words & Music by
Björk Gudmundsdóttir, Margrét Örnalfssdóttir, Einar Örn Benediktsson, Thor Eldon,
Bragi Ólafsson & Sigtryggur Balduresson

C   **F**   **C/G**   **Dm**

Intro

| C | F | C | F |
| C | F | C | F |

Verse 1

C C/G   Dm
She lives in this house over there,
C   C/G   Dm
Has her world outside it.
C C/G   Dm
Scrabbles in the earth with her fingers
C   C/G   Dm
And her mouth, she's five years old.
C   C/G   Dm
Threads worms on a string,
C   C/G   Dm
Keeps spiders in her pocket.
C   C/G   Dm
Collects fly-wings in a jar,
C   C/G   Dm
Scrubs horse-flies and, and pinches them on a line.

Chorus 1

C   F
Oh,_____
C   F
Oh,___ hee.
C   F
Oh,_____
C   F
Oh..._____

Verse 2

C C/G   Dm
She has one friend - he lives next door,
C   C/G   Dm
They're listening to the weather.
C C/G   Dm
He knows how many freckles she's got,
C   C/G   Dm
She scratches his beard.

```
         C      C/G           Dm
         She's painting huge books,
         C      C/G         Dm
         And glues them together.
         C      C/G       Dm
         They saw a big raven,
         C      C/G           Dm                  (C)
         It glided down the sky, she touched it.
```

Chorus 2   As Chorus 1

Instrumental | C   C/G | Dm | C   C/G | Dm   ‖

```
         C      C/G       Dm
```
Verse 3   Today is her birthday,
```
         C            C/G       Dm
         They're smoking cigars.
         C         C/G         Dm
         He's got a chain of flowers,
         C        C/G       Dm
         And sews a bird   in her knickers.
```

Chorus 3   As Chorus 1

Coda | C   C/G | Dm   ‖

```
         C            C/G       Dm
         They're smoking cigars,
         C         C/G   Dm
         They lie in    the bathtub,
         C      C/G       Dm
         A chain of    flowers.
         C              C/G
Dan, dan, dan, dan, ba-dan,
Dm
Dan, dan, dan, dan, dan, ba-dan.
C              C/G
Dan, dan, dan, dan, ba-dan, dan,
Dm                        C
Dan, dan, dan, dan, ba-dan, dan.
```

THE SONICS: Psycho

Words & Music by
Gerald Roslie

C   F   G   C#   F#   G*

Intro | Drums | Drums N.C. ‖
Wow!

Chorus 1
C   F G   F   C   F | G F |
Baby   you're driving me crazy,
C   F G   F   C   F | G F |
I said, baby,   you're driving me crazy.

Verse 1
C   F | G F |
Oh, well you turn me on,
C   F | G F |
Then you shut me down
C   F | G F |
Oh well tell me baby
C   F | G F |
Am I just your clown?
| G | F | N.C. | N.C.   ‖
Psycho!   Wow!   Wow!

Chorus 2
C   F G   F   C   F | G F |
Baby   you're driving me crazy,
C   F   G F   C   F | G F |
I said I'm losing my mind,   you treat me so un - kind.
| G | F | N.C. | N.C.   ‖
Psycho!   Wow!   Wow!

Solo ‖: C F | G F | C F | G F :‖
| G | F | N.C. | N.C.   ‖
Wow!   Wow!

Chorus 3
C   F G   F   C   F | G F |
Baby   you're driving me crazy,
C   F   G F   C   F | G F |
I'm going out of my head   and now I wish I was dead.
| G | F | N.C. | N.C.   ‖
Psycho!   Wow!   Wow!

Chorus 4
C#   F# G#   F#   C#   F# | G# F# |
Baby   you're driving me crazy,
C#   F#   G# F#   C#   F# | G# F# ‖
I'm going out of my head   now I wish I was dead.   Wow!

Outro ‖: C# F# | G#   F# :‖ *Repeat to fade*
Psycho!   Wow!

170

SUICIDAL TENDENCIES: Institutionalized

Words & Music by
Michael Muir & Louis Mayorga

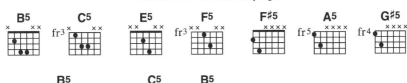

B5   C5   B5

Verse 1   Sometimes I try to do things,

C5 cont. sim.

And it just doesn't work out the way I wanted to.
I get real frustrated and I try hard to do it ,
And I take my time and it doesn't work out the way I wanted to.
It's like I concentrate real hard and it doesn't work out,
Everything I do and everything I try never turns out.
It's like I need time to figure these things out,
But there's always someone there going.
"Hey Mike,
You know we've been noticing,
You've been having a lot of problems lately.
You know, maybe you should get away,
And like, maybe you should talk about it,
You'll feel a lot better."
And I go, "No it's okay, you know, I'll figure it out,
Just leave me alone I'll figure it out.
You know I'll just work by myself."
And they go,
"Well you know, if you want to talk about it,
I'll be here you know,
And you'll probably feel a lot better if you talk about it."
And I go,
"No I don't want to I'm okay,
I'll figure it out myself"
And they just keep bugging me,
And they just keep bugging me,
And it builds up inside and it builds up inside.

                     B5 E5 B5   C5 F5 C5

Pre-chorus 1   So you're gon - na be institutional - ized,

              B5   E5   B5   C5   F5 C5

You'll come out brain - washed with bloodshot eyes.

B5   E5   B5 C5 F5 C5

You won't have any say,

             B5   E5 B5   C5   F5 C5

They'll brainwash you until you see their way.

Chorus 1

   F#5   A5   G#5
I'm not crazy, insti - tutionalized.

F#5   A5   G#5
You're the one who's crazy, insti - tutionalized.

    F#5   A5   G#5
You're driving me crazy, insti - tutionalized.

   B5   E5 B5 C5   F5 C5
They stick me in an   insti - tu - tion,

B5   E5 B5 C5   F5 C5
Said it was the only so - lu - tion.

    B5   E5   B5   C5   F5 C5
To give me the need - ed pro - fessional help,

      B5   E5   B5 C5 F5 C5   B5
To pro - tect me from the ene - my, my - self.

Verse 2

B5   C5   B5   C5 cont. sim.
   I was in my room and I was just like staring at the wall,
Thinking about everything,but then again,
I was thinking about nothing.
And then my mom came in, and I didn't even know she was there,
She called my name, and I didn't even hear it,
And then she started screaming, "Mike! Mike!"
And I go, what, "What's the matter?"
And she goes, "What's the matter with you?"
I go, "There's nothing wrong Mom."
And she goes, "Don't tell me that, you're on drugs!"
And I go, "No Mom, I'm not on drugs I'm okay,
I was just thinking you know? Why don't you get me a Pepsi?"
And she goes, "No, you're on drugs!"
I go, "Mom I'm okay, I'm just thinking."
She goes, "No, you're not thinking, you're on drugs!
Normal people don't act that way! "
I go, "Mom, just give me a Pepsi please, all I want is a Pepsi."
And she wouldn't give it to me.
All I wanted was a Pepsi, just one Pepsi,
And she wouldn't give it to me.
Just a Pepsi.

Pre-chorus 2

   B5   E5   B5 C5 F5   C5
They give you a white shirt with long sleeves,

B5   E5   B5   C5   F5   C5
Tied around your back, you're treated like thieves.

B5   E5 B5 C5   F5 C5
Drug you up be - cause they're la - zy,

B5   E5   B5 C5   F5   C5
It's too much work to help a crazy.

Chorus 2   As Chorus 1

	B5	C5	B5	C5 cont. sim.

Verse 3   I was sitting in my room, and my mom and my dad came in,
And they pulled up a chair and they sat down, they go,
"Mike, we need to talk to you."
And I go, "Okay, what's the matter?"
They go, "Me and your mom have been noticing lately,
That you've been having a lot of problems,
You've been going off for no reason,
And we're afraid you're gonna hurt somebody,
We're afraid you're gonna hurt yourself.
So we decided that it would be in your interest,
If we put you somewhere,
Where you could get the help that you need."
And I go, "Wait, what are you talking about?
We decided? My best interest?
How can you know what my best interest is?
How can you say what my best interest is?
What are you trying to say, I'm crazy?
When I went to your schools, I went to your churches,
I went to your institutional learning facilities.
So how can you say I'm crazy?"

            B5   E5   B5 C5   F5   C5

Pre-chorus 3   They say they're gon - na fix my brain,

            B5   E5   B5 C5   F5   C5

Al - leviate suffer - ing and my pain.

B5   E5   B5 C5   F5   C5

But by the time they fix my head,

B5   E5 B5 C5   F5   C5

Mental - ly   I'll be dead.

Chorus 3   As Chorus 1

It doesn't matter I'll probably get hit by a car anyway.

SUICIDE: Dream Baby Dream

Words & Music by
Alan Vega & Martin Reverby

Eadd9   E   E/A   A   A/B   B

Intro ‖: Eadd9 E | E | E/A A | A/B B :‖

Verse 1
Eadd9   E   E/A   A   A/B B
Dream baby dream, dream baby dream,
Eadd9   E   E/A   A   A/B B
Dream baby dream, dream baby dream,
    Eadd9 E
Forev - er.

Link 1 | E/A A | A/B B ‖

‖: Eadd9 E | E | E/A A | A/B B :‖

Verse 2
Eadd9   E   E/A A A/B B
Keep those dreams burnin' baby,
Eadd9   E   E/A A A/B B
Keep my dreams burnin' forever.
Eadd9   E   E/A A A/B B
Dream baby dream,
Eadd9   E   E/A A A/B B
Dream baby dream,
    Eadd9 E
Forev - er.

Link 2   As Link 1

Verse 3
Eadd9   E   E/A   A   A/B B
Dream baby dream, dream baby dream,
Eadd9   E   E/A   A   A/B B
Dream baby dream, dream baby dream,
    Eadd9 E
Forev - er.

Link 3   As Link 1

Verse 4
Eadd9   E
Dream baby dream,
E/A   A   A/B B
Babe you gotta keep those dreams burnin',
Eadd9   E   E/A A A/B B
Keep those dreams burn - in', forever.

Eadd9   **E**
Dream baby dream, dream baby dream,

E/A   **A** **A/B**   **B**
Dream baby dream, dream baby dream,

Eadd9   **E**
Dream ba - by, dream baby, dream baby, dream baby,

E/A   **A** **A/B B**
Dream ba - by,

Eadd9   **E**
Dream baby, dream.

Link 4   As Link 1

     Eadd9   **E**   **E/A A A/B B**
Verse 5 Ah you keep that flame burnin' baby,

       Eadd9   **E**   **E/A A A/B B**
    You gotta keep that flame burn - in' forever, baby.

     Eadd9   **E**
    Dream baby dream,

                 E/A A A/B B
    Yeah come baby keep those dreams burnin',

      Eadd9 E   **E/A** **A A/B B**
    Forev - er, and ev - er,

      Eadd9 E   **E/A** **A A/B B**
    Forev - er, and ev - er,

     Eadd9   **E**
    Oh, dream baby, dream.

Link 5   As Link 1

       Eadd9   **E**
Verse 6 It's those dreams that keep you free baby,

    E/A   **A**   **A/B B**
    Yeah you gotta make them dreams come true.

    Eadd9   **E**
    Keep those dreams burnin' baby,

    E/A   **A**   **A/B B**
    Keep them dreams burning forever.

    Eadd9   **E**
    Dream ba - by, dream baby, dream baby, dream baby,

    E/A   **A**   **A/B** **B**
    Dream ba - by, dream baby, dream baby,

      Eadd9 E   **E/A** **A A/B B**
    Forev - er, and ev - er,

      Eadd9 E   **E/A** **A A/B B**
    Forev - er, and ev - er,

    Eadd9   **E**
    Dream baby dream.

                       Play 3 times

Link 6 | **E/A A** | **A/B B** |: **Eadd9 E** | **E** | | **E/A A** | **A/B B** :|

     Eadd9   **E** **E/A A A/B B**
Outro |: Dream baby dream.   :| *Ad lib. to end*

                            175

TALKING HEADS: Once In A Lifetime

Words & Music by
David Byrne, Brian Eno, Jerry Harrison, Tina Weymouth & Christopher Frantz

A7sus4   A7sus4/F♯   D   D/F♯   G   G/A   D/A   C

Intro ‖: A7sus4 | A7sus4/F♯ | A7sus4 | A7sus4/F♯ :‖

Verse 1

A7sus4
And you may find yourself
A7sus4/F♯
living in a shotgun shack
A7sus4
And you may find yourself
A7sus4/F♯
In another part of the world
A7sus4
And you may find yourself
A7sus4/F♯   A7sus4
behind the wheel of a large au - tomobile

          A7sus4/F♯
And you may find yourself in a beautiful house,
A7sus4   A7sus4/F♯
With a beauti - ful wife
                A7sus4
And you may ask yourself... well...
A7sus4/F♯   A7sus4
How did I get here?

Chorus 1

          D   D/F♯ G
Letting the days go by let the water hold me down
G/A   D   D/F♯ G
Letting the days go by water flowing underground
G/A   D   D/F♯   G
Into the blue again after the money's gone
G/A   D   D/F♯ G
Once in a lifetime water flowing underground.

Verse 2

A⁷sus⁴
And you may ask yourself

A⁷sus⁴/F♯
How do I work this?

A⁷sus⁴
And you may ask yourself

A⁷sus⁴/F♯
Where is that large automobile?

A⁷sus⁴
And you may tell yourself

A⁷sus⁴/F♯
This is not my beautiful house!

A⁷sus⁴
And you may tell yourself

A⁷sus⁴/F♯   **A⁷sus⁴**
This is not my beautiful wife!

Chorus 2

          D   **D/F♯** **G**
Letting the days go by let the water hold me down

G/A   **D**   **D/F♯** **G**
Letting the days go by water flowing underground

G/A   **D**   **D/F♯**   **G**
Into the blue again after the money's gone

G/A   **D**   **D/F♯** **G**
Once in a lifetime water flowing underground.

Bridge

   D/A   **D/F♯**
‖:   Same as it ever was...   same as it ever was... :‖ *Play 4 times*

A⁷sus⁴   **A⁷sus⁴/F♯**
Water dissolving   and water removing

A⁷sus⁴   **A⁷sus⁴/F♯**
There is water at the bottom of the ocean

              A⁷sus⁴
Under the water   carry the water

A⁷sus⁴/F♯   **A⁷sus⁴ A⁷sus⁴/F♯ A⁷sus⁴**
Remove the water at the bottom of the ocean!

Chorus 3

          D   **D/F♯** **G**
Letting the days go by let the water hold me down

G/A   **D**   **D/F♯** **G**
Letting the days go by water flowing underground

G/A   **D**   **D/F♯**   **G**
Into the blue again into the silent water

G/A   **D**   **D/F♯** **G**
Under the rocks and stones there is water underground.

G/A   **D**   **D/F♯** **G**
Letting the days go by let the water hold me down.

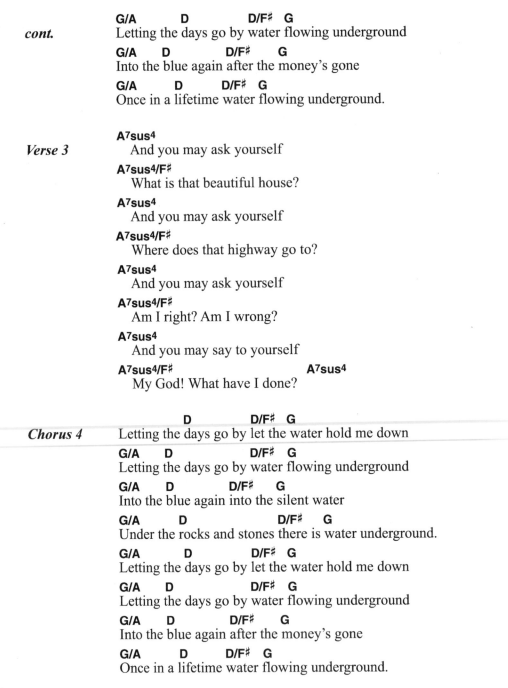

cont.

G/A   D   D/F♯ G
Letting the days go by water flowing underground

G/A   D   D/F♯ G
Into the blue again after the money's gone

G/A   D   D/F♯ G
Once in a lifetime water flowing underground.

Verse 3

A⁷sus4
 And you may ask yourself

A⁷sus4/F♯
 What is that beautiful house?

A⁷sus4
 And you may ask yourself

A⁷sus4/F♯
 Where does that highway go to?

A⁷sus4
 And you may ask yourself

A⁷sus4/F♯
 Am I right? Am I wrong?

A⁷sus4
 And you may say to yourself

A⁷sus4/F♯   A⁷sus4
 My God! What have I done?

Chorus 4

      D   D/F♯ G
Letting the days go by let the water hold me down

G/A   D   D/F♯ G
Letting the days go by water flowing underground

G/A   D   D/F♯ G
Into the blue again into the silent water

G/A   D   D/F♯ G
Under the rocks and stones there is water underground.

G/A   D   D/F♯ G
Letting the days go by let the water hold me down

G/A   D   D/F♯ G
Letting the days go by water flowing underground

G/A   D   D/F♯ G
Into the blue again after the money's gone

G/A   D   D/F♯ G
Once in a lifetime water flowing underground.

Chorus 4

 D   C   G
‖: Same as it ever was... same as it ever was... :‖ *Repeat to fade*

TELEVISION: Marquee Moon

Words & Music by
Tom Verlaine

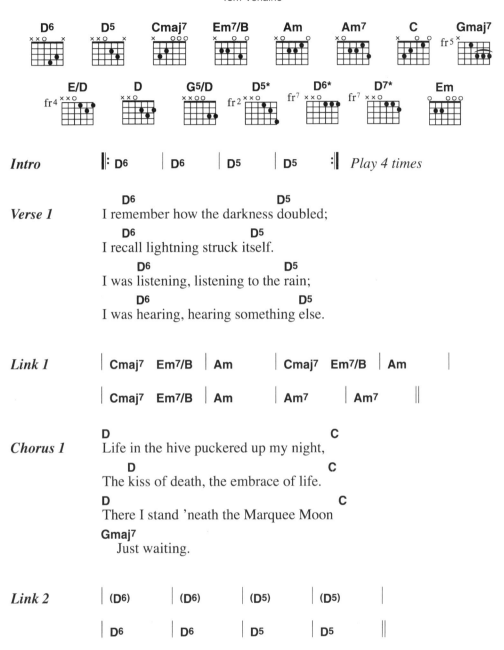

Intro   ‖: D6 | D6 | D5 | D5 :‖ *Play 4 times*

Verse 1

      D6   D5
I remember how the darkness doubled;
     D6   D5
I recall lightning struck itself.
       D6   D5
I was listening, listening to the rain;
       D6   D5
I was hearing, hearing something else.

Link 1 | Cmaj7 Em7/B | Am | Cmaj7 Em7/B | Am |

| Cmaj7 Em7/B | Am | Am7 | Am7   ‖

Chorus 1

D   C
Life in the hive puckered up my night,
     D   C
The kiss of death, the embrace of life.
D   C
There I stand 'neath the Marquee Moon
Gmaj7
   Just waiting.

Link 2 | (D6) | (D6) | (D5) | (D5) |

| D6 | D6 | D5 | D5 ‖

Verse 2

D6   D5
I spoke to a man down at the tracks

     D6   D5
And I ask him how he don't go mad?

         D6   D5
He said, "Look here, Junior, don't you be so happy,

     D6   D5
And for heaven's sake, don't you be so sad."

Link 3

| Cmaj7 Em7/B | Am | Cmaj7 Em7/B | Am | |

| Cmaj7 Em7/B | Am | Am7 | Am7 ||

Chorus 2

D   C
Life in the hive puckered up my night,

     D   C
The kiss of death, the embrace of life.

D   C
Outside 'neath the Marquee Moon

Gmaj7
    Hesitating.

Guitar solo

| D | D C | D | D C |

| D | D C | Gmaj7 | Gmaj7 ||

Link 4

| D6 | D6 | D5 | D5 ||

Verse 3

         D6   D5
Well a Cadillac, it pulled out of the graveyard,

         D6   D5
Pulled up to me, and they said,"Get in, get in."

           D6   D5
Then the Cadillac, it puttered back into the graveyard,

     D6   D5
And me, I got out again.

Link 5

| Cmaj7 Em7/B | Am | Cmaj7 Em7/B | Am | |

| Cmaj7 Em7/B | Am | Am7 | Am7 ||

180

Chorus 3

D   C
Life in the hive puckered up my night,

        D   C
The kiss of death, the embrace of life.

D   C
Outside 'neath the Marquee Moon

Gmaj7
   But I ain't waiting, uh-uh.

Link 6

$\|$: D6 | D6 | D5 | D5   :$\|$ *Play 3 times*

Bridge solo

$\|$: D6 | D6 | D5 | D5   :$\|$ *Play 26 times*

| D5 | D5 | E/D | E/D | D | D |

| G5/D | G5/D | D5* | D5* | D6* | D6* |

| D7* | D7* $\|$: D | D | D6 | D6   :$\|$

| Em | Em | D6 | D6 | C | C |

| D | D | D $\|$

Link 7

| Drums $\|$ (D6) | (D6) | (D5) | (D5) |

| D6 | D6 | D5 | D5 $\|$

Verse 4

   D6   D5
I remember how the darkness doubled;

   D6   D5
I recall lightning struck itself.

     D6   D5
I was listening, listening to the rain;

     D6   D5
I was hearing, hearing something else.

Link 8

| Cmaj7 Em7/B | Am | Cmaj7 Em7/B | Am |

| Cmaj7 Em7/B | Am | Am7 | Am7 | D $\|$

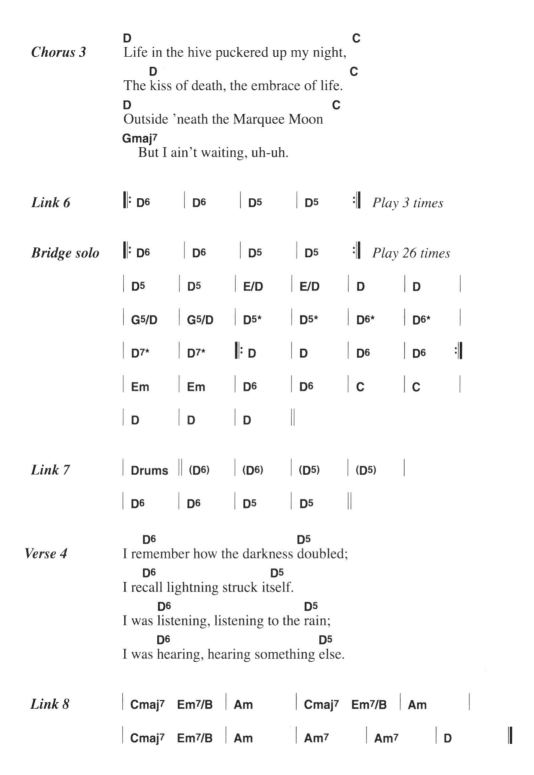

TEENAGE FANCLUB: The Concept

Words & Music by
Gerard Love, Norman Blake & Raymond McGinley

G   G/F♯   Em7   Am7   D   G7   A

A6   Dsus4   Bm   Em   Am   C   Csus2

Verse 1

     G   **G/F♯**
She wears denim, wher - ever she goes.
           Em7
Says she's gonna get some records, by the Status Quo.
    Am7 D
Oh yeah,
    G   **G/F♯**
Oh yeah.
        G   **G/F♯**
Still she won't be forced, a - gainst her will.
     Em7
Says she don't do drugs, but she does the pill.
    Am7 D
Oh yeah,
    G   **G7**
Oh yeah.

Chorus 1

   Am7   **D**   **G G/F♯ Em7**
I didn't want to hurt you, oh—— yeah.
   Am7   **D**   **G G/F♯ Em7**
I didn't want to hurt you, oh—— yeah.

Link 1

| **A A6 A A6** | **A A6 A A6** | **Am7** | **Dsus4** | **Dsus4**   ‖

Verse 2

     G   **G/F♯**
Says she likes my hair, 'cause it's down my back.
      Em7
Says she likes the group, 'cause we pull in the slack.
    Am7 D
Oh yeah,
    G   **G/F♯**
Oh yeah.

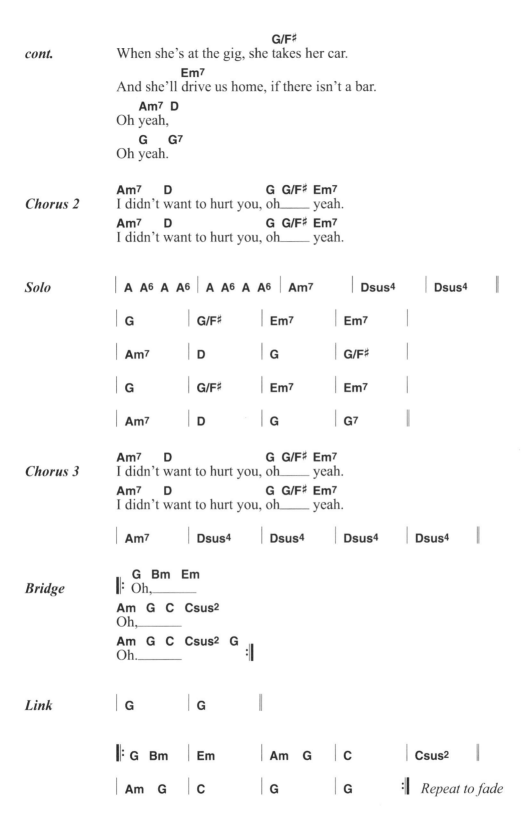

                              G/F♯

cont.   When she's at the gig, she takes her car.

                Em⁷
And she'll drive us home, if there isn't a bar.

      Am⁷ D
Oh yeah,

      G   G⁷
Oh yeah.

      Am⁷   D   **G G/F♯ Em⁷**
Chorus 2   I didn't want to hurt you, oh____ yeah.

      Am⁷   D   **G G/F♯ Em⁷**
I didn't want to hurt you, oh____ yeah.

Solo | **A A⁶ A A⁶** | **A A⁶ A A⁶** | **Am⁷** | **Dsus⁴** | **Dsus⁴**   ‖

      | **G** | **G/F♯** | **Em⁷** | **Em⁷** |

      | **Am⁷** | **D** | **G** | **G/F♯** |

      | **G** | **G/F♯** | **Em⁷** | **Em⁷** |

      | **Am⁷** | **D** | **G** | **G⁷**   ‖

      Am⁷   D   **G G/F♯ Em⁷**
Chorus 3   I didn't want to hurt you, oh____ yeah.

      Am⁷   D   **G G/F♯ Em⁷**
I didn't want to hurt you, oh____ yeah.

      | **Am⁷** | **Dsus⁴** | **Dsus⁴** | **Dsus⁴** | **Dsus⁴**   ‖

        G Bm Em
Bridge   ‖: Oh,_____

      Am G C Csus²
Oh,_____

      Am G C Csus² G
Oh._____   :‖

Link | **G** | **G**   ‖

      ‖: **G Bm** | **Em** | **Am G** | **C** | **Csus²**   ‖

      | **Am G** | **C** | **G** | **G**   :‖ *Repeat to fade*

THE THE: Uncertain Smile

Words & Music by
Matt Johnson

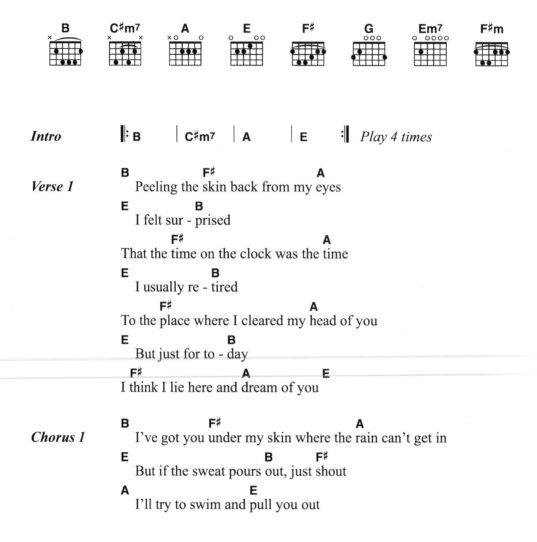

Intro ‖: B | C#m7 | A | E :‖ *Play 4 times*

Verse 1

B   F#   A
    Peeling the skin back from my eyes

E   B
    I felt sur - prised

       F#   A
That the time on the clock was the time

E   B
    I usually re - tired

       F#   A
To the place where I cleared my head of you

E   B
    But just for to - day

   F#   A   E
I think I lie here and dream of you

Chorus 1

B   F#   A
    I've got you under my skin where the rain can't get in

E   B   F#
    But if the sweat pours out, just shout

A   E
    I'll try to swim and pull you out

| Link 1 | ‖: G | F♯ | G | A :‖ |

| | ‖: Em7 | F♯ | G | A :‖ |

| Bridge | ‖: A | A | G | G :‖ |

| | | F♯ | F♯ | E | E ‖ |

Verse 2

B   F♯   A   E
A howling wind blows the litter as the rain flows
B   F♯   A
As street lamps pour orange coloured shapes
                E
Through your   windows
B   F♯   A   E
A broken soul stares from a pair of watering eyes
B   F♯   A   E
Uncertain e - motions force an   uncertain   smile

| Link 2 | | B | F♯ | A | E ‖ |

| Chorus 2 | As Chorus 1 |

| Link 3 | ‖: G | F♯ | G | A :‖ | *Play 4 times* |

| Instr. | ‖: Em7 | F♯m | G | A :‖ | *Repeat to fade* |

185

THERAPY?: Screamager

Words & Music by
Fyfe Ewing, Andrew Cairns & Michael McKeegan

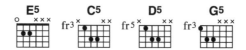

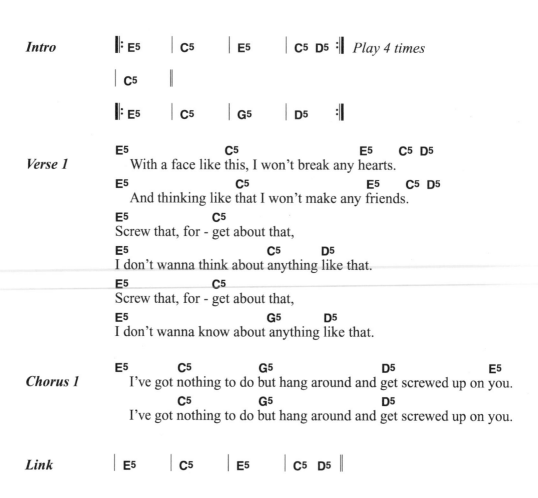

Intro ‖: E5 | C5 | E5 | C5 D5 :‖ *Play 4 times*

| C5 ‖

‖: E5 | C5 | G5 | D5 :‖

Verse 1

E5   C5   E5   C5 D5
    With a face like this, I won't break any hearts.

E5   C5   E5   C5 D5
    And thinking like that I won't make any friends.

E5   C5
Screw that, for - get about that,

E5   C5   D5
I don't wanna think about anything like that.

E5   C5
Screw that, for - get about that,

E5   G5   D5
I don't wanna know about anything like that.

Chorus 1

E5   C5   G5   D5   E5
    I've got nothing to do but hang around and get screwed up on you.

            C5   G5   D5
    I've got nothing to do but hang around and get screwed up on you.

Link | E5 | C5 | E5 | C5 D5 ‖

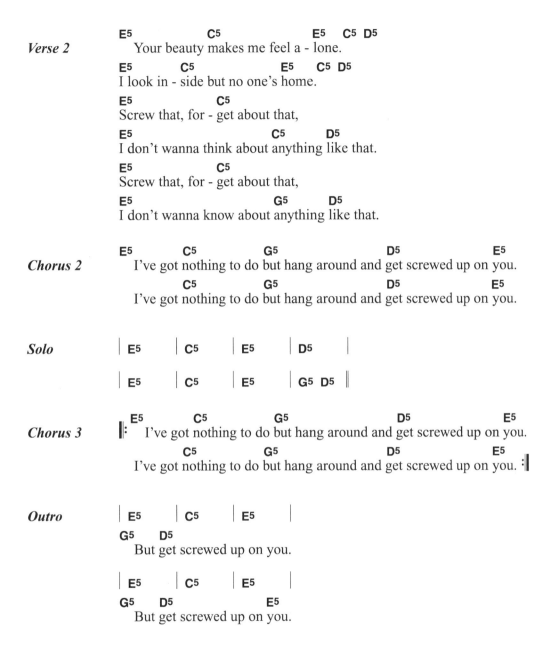

Verse 2

E5   C5   E5   C5 D5
Your beauty makes me feel a - lone.

E5   C5   E5   C5 D5
I look in - side but no one's home.

E5   C5
Screw that, for - get about that,

E5   C5   D5
I don't wanna think about anything like that.

E5   C5
Screw that, for - get about that,

E5   G5   D5
I don't wanna know about anything like that.

Chorus 2

E5   C5   G5   D5   E5
I've got nothing to do but hang around and get screwed up on you.

C5   G5   D5   E5
I've got nothing to do but hang around and get screwed up on you.

Solo

| E5 | C5 | E5 | D5 | |

| E5 | C5 | E5 | G5 D5 ‖

Chorus 3

E5   C5   G5   D5   E5
‖: I've got nothing to do but hang around and get screwed up on you.

C5   G5   D5   E5
I've got nothing to do but hang around and get screwed up on you. :‖

Outro

| E5 | C5 | E5 | |

G5   D5
But get screwed up on you.

| E5 | C5 | E5 | |

G5   D5   E5
But get screwed up on you.

THE THIRTEENTH FLOOR ELEVATORS:
You're Gonna Miss Me

Words & Music by
Roky Erickson

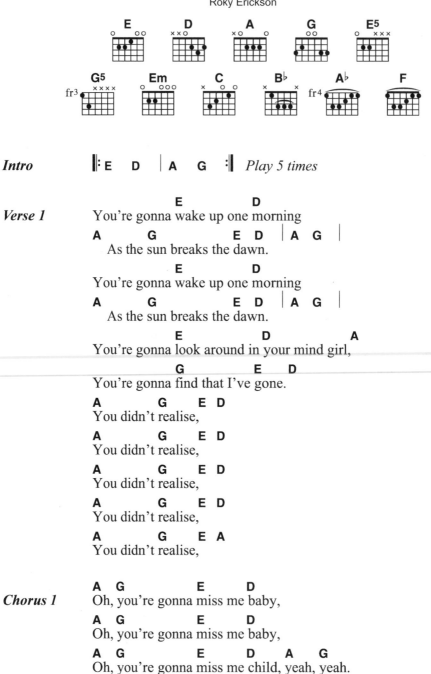

Intro   ‖: E   D | A   G :‖ *Play 5 times*

Verse 1
　　　　　　　　　　　　　E　　　　　D
　　You're gonna wake up one morning
　A　　　G　　　　　　E D | A G |
　　As the sun breaks the dawn.
　　　　　　　　　　　　　E　　　　　D
　　You're gonna wake up one morning
　A　　　G　　　　　　　E D | A G |
　　As the sun breaks the dawn.
　　　　　　　　　　　　E　　　　　D　　　　　A
　　You're gonna look around in your mind girl,
　　　　　　　　　　　　G　　　　E　　D
　　You're gonna find that I've gone.
　A　　　　G　　　E D
　　You didn't realise,
　A　　　　G　　　E D
　　You didn't realise,
　A　　　　G　　　E D
　　You didn't realise,
　A　　　　G　　　E D
　　You didn't realise,
　A　　　　G　　　E A
　　You didn't realise,

Chorus 1
　A G　　　　E　　　D
　　Oh, you're gonna miss me baby,
　A G　　　　E　　　D
　　Oh, you're gonna miss me baby,
　A G　　　　E　　　D　　A　　G
　　Oh, you're gonna miss me child, yeah, yeah.

Link 1 | Em5 | Em5 | Em5 G5 | Em5 G5 ‖

Bridge

   Em **G5 Em** **G5**
I gave you the warning,

   Em **G5** **Em** **G5**
But you never heeded it,

   Em   **G5 Em**   **G5**
How can you say you miss my loving

   Em **G5** **Em** **G5**
When you never needed it.

Link 2 | Em   G5 | Em   G5 | Em | Em   ‖

Verse 2

   C   **B♭**
You're gonna wake up wondering,

   A♭   **B♭**
 Find yourself all a - lone,

   C   **B♭**
No-one's gonna stop you baby,

   F   **D**
I'm not coming home,

   F   **D**
I'm not coming home,

   F   **D** | **D** | **E** | **E** ‖
I'm not coming home.

Outro ‖: **E** | **D** | **A** | **G** :‖ *Repeat to fade*
   w/ad lib. vocals

189

THROWING MUSES: Bright Yellow Gun

Words & Music by
Kristin Hersh

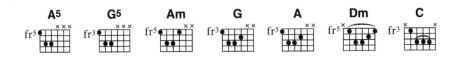

A5   G5   Am   G   A   Dm   C

Verse 1

    N.C   A5   G5
With your bright yellow gun,
A5   G5
  You own the sun,
N.C A5   G5   A5   G5
And I think I need a little poison.
Am   G
  To keep me tame,
A   G
  Keep me awake,
    Am   G   A   G
I have nothing to offer but confusion.
      Am   G
And the circus in my head,
      Am   G
In the middle of the bed.
      Am   G
In the middle of the night,
N.C   A5   G5
With your bright silver frown.
A5   G5
  You own the town,
N.C Am   G   A   G   N.C
And I think I need a little poison.
Am   G
  I have no secrets,
A   G
  I have no lies,
      Am   G   Am   G
I have nothing to offer but the middle of the night.
N.C A5   G5   A5   G5   N.C
And I think you need a little poison.

Instrumental 1 ‖: Dm | C | Dm | C   :‖

Verse 2

          Dm   C   Dm   C
You need one apple a week to survive,

             Dm   C   Dm   C
And you still have to ask if you're alive,

             Dm   C   Dm   C
You have nothing to offer but police my dreams.

Dm   C
   Keep me clean,

Dm   C
   Keep me awake.

           Dm   C
With your bright yellow gun

Dm   C
   You own the sun,

       Dm   C   Dm   C
And I think I need a little poison.

           Dm   C
With your bright silver grin,

Dm   C
   You own sin,

       Dm   C   Dm   C
And I think I need a little poison,

       Dm   C   Dm   C
And I think I need a little poison,

       Dm   C   Dm   C
And I think I need a little poison.

Instrumental 2 ‖: Dm | C | Dm | C   :‖

Coda

Dm   C   Dm   C
Bright yellow gun,

Dm   C   Dm   C
Bright yellow gun,

Dm   C   Dm   C
Bright yellow gun,

Dm   C   Dm   C
Bright yellow gun,

Dm   C   Dm   C
Bright yellow gun,

Dm   C   Dm   A5
Bright yellow gun.

THE UNDERTONES: Teenage Kicks

Words & Music by
John O'Neill

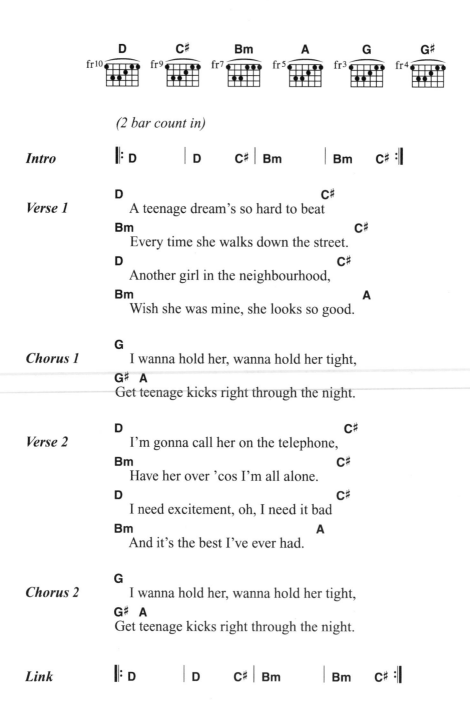

(2 bar count in)

Intro ‖: D | D C♯ | Bm | Bm C♯ :‖

Verse 1

D   C♯
A teenage dream's so hard to beat
Bm   C♯
Every time she walks down the street.
D   C♯
Another girl in the neighbourhood,
Bm   A
Wish she was mine, she looks so good.

Chorus 1

G
I wanna hold her, wanna hold her tight,
G♯ A
Get teenage kicks right through the night.

Verse 2

D   C♯
I'm gonna call her on the telephone,
Bm   C♯
Have her over 'cos I'm all alone.
D   C♯
I need excitement, oh, I need it bad
Bm   A
And it's the best I've ever had.

Chorus 2

G
I wanna hold her, wanna hold her tight,
G♯ A
Get teenage kicks right through the night.

Link ‖: D | D C♯ | Bm | Bm C♯ :‖

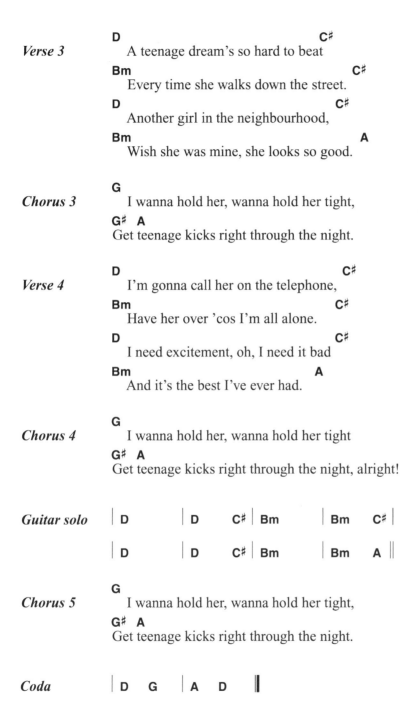

Verse 3

D   C♯
A teenage dream's so hard to beat

Bm   C♯
Every time she walks down the street.

D   C♯
Another girl in the neighbourhood,

Bm   A
Wish she was mine, she looks so good.

Chorus 3

G
I wanna hold her, wanna hold her tight,

G♯ A
Get teenage kicks right through the night.

Verse 4

D   C♯
I'm gonna call her on the telephone,

Bm   C♯
Have her over 'cos I'm all alone.

D   C♯
I need excitement, oh, I need it bad

Bm   A
And it's the best I've ever had.

Chorus 4

G
I wanna hold her, wanna hold her tight

G♯ A
Get teenage kicks right through the night, alright!

Guitar solo

| D | D   C♯| Bm | Bm   C♯|

| D | D   C♯| Bm | Bm   A ‖

Chorus 5

G
I wanna hold her, wanna hold her tight,

G♯ A
Get teenage kicks right through the night.

Coda

| D G | A D ‖

THE VELVET UNDERGROUND: Sunday Morning

Words & Music by
Lou Reed & John Cale

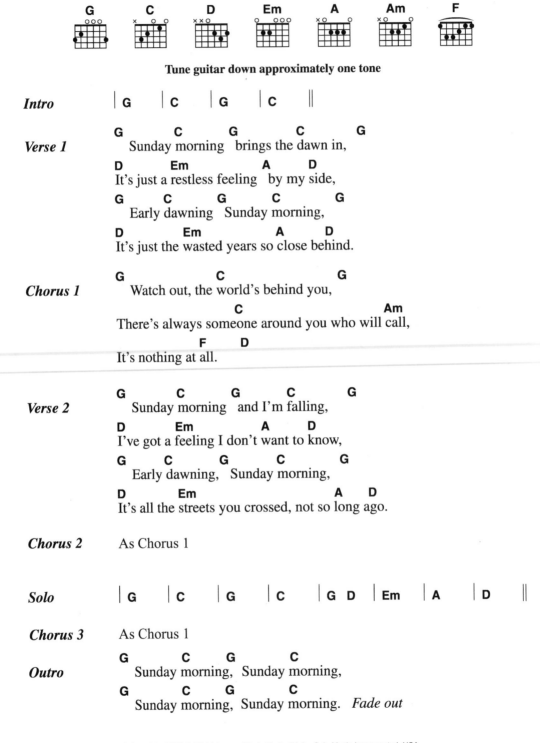

Tune guitar down approximately one tone

Intro
| G | C | G | C ‖

Verse 1
```
      G        C       G        C        G
     Sunday morning   brings the dawn in,
     D        Em            A       D
     It's just a restless feeling   by my side,
      G       C       G        C        G
       Early dawning   Sunday morning,
     D          Em           A       D
     It's just the wasted years so close behind.
```

Chorus 1
```
      G                 C              G
       Watch out, the world's behind you,
                        C                     Am
     There's always someone around you who will call,
                 F       D
     It's nothing at all.
```

Verse 2
```
      G       C       G       C       G
       Sunday morning   and I'm falling,
     D        Em           A       D
     I've got a feeling I don't want to know,
      G       C       G       C        G
        Early dawning,   Sunday morning,
     D          Em                  A       D
     It's all the streets you crossed, not so long ago.
```

Chorus 2   As Chorus 1

Solo
| G | C | G | C | G D | Em | A | D ‖

Chorus 3   As Chorus 1

Outro
```
      G        C      G        C
     Sunday morning,  Sunday morning,
      G        C      G        C
     Sunday morning, Sunday morning.   Fade out
```

VIOLENT FEMMES: Blister In The Sun

Words & Music by
Gordon Gano

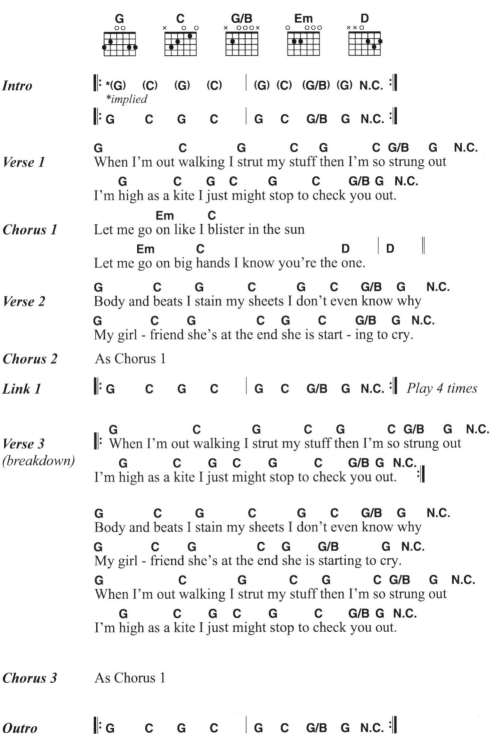

Intro

‖: *(G) (C) (G) (C) | (G) (C) (G/B) (G) N.C. :‖
implied

‖: G   C   G   C | G   C   G/B   G   N.C. :‖

Verse 1

```
   G          C        G        C    G      C   G/B  G   N.C.
When I'm out walking I strut my stuff then I'm so strung out
   G       C   G  C   G      C      G/B G  N.C.
I'm high as a kite I just might stop to check you out.
```

Chorus 1

```
             Em      C
Let me go on like I blister in the sun
      Em        C                    D    | D     ‖
Let me go on big hands I know you're the one.
```

Verse 2

```
G       C   G       C        G    C   G/B  G     N.C.
Body and beats I stain my sheets I don't even know why
G        C   G        C  G   C    G/B  G   N.C.
My girl - friend she's at the end she is start - ing to cry.
```

Chorus 2

As Chorus 1

Link 1

‖: G   C   G   C | G   C   G/B   G   N.C. :‖ *Play 4 times*

**Verse 3
(breakdown)**

```
      G          C        G        C    G      C   G/B  G   N.C.
‖: When I'm out walking I strut my stuff then I'm so strung out
   G       C   G  C   G      C      G/B G  N.C.
I'm high as a kite I just might stop to check you out.    :‖
```

```
G       C   G       C        G    C   G/B  G     N.C.
Body and beats I stain my sheets I don't even know why
G        C   G        C  G   G/B           G   N.C.
My girl - friend she's at the end she is starting to cry.
G          C        G        C    G      C   G/B  G   N.C.
When I'm out walking I strut my stuff then I'm so strung out
   G       C   G  C   G      C      G/B G  N.C.
I'm high as a kite I just might stop to check you out.
```

Chorus 3

As Chorus 1

Outro

‖: G   C   G   C | G   C   G/B   G   N.C. :‖

VISAGE: Fade to Grey

Words & Music by
Billy Currie, Midge Ure & Christopher Payne

E   Am   C   Em   Dm   F

Intro

| E | E | E | Am | |
| Am | Am | Am | Am ‖
‖: C | Em | Am | Am :‖

Devenions gris.

Verse 1

Dm   F
One man on a lonely platform,
                                   Am
One case sitting by his side.
Dm   F
Two eyes staring cold and silent,
                              Am
Show fear as he turns to hide.

Chorus 1

C   Em   Am
Ah,___ we fade to grey, fade to grey.
C   Em   Am
Ah,___ we fade to grey, fade to grey.

Verse 2

Dm   F
Un homme dans une gare isolée,
                                   Am
Une valise à ses cô - tés.
Dm   F
Deux yeux fixes et froids
                                      Am
Montrent de la peur lors - qu'il se tourne pour se cacher.

Chorus 2

C   Em   Am
Ah,___ we fade to grey, fade to grey.
C   Em   Am
Ah,___ we fade to grey, fade to grey.

Bridge

Am
Sens la pluie comme un été anglais,

Entends les notes d'une chanson lointaine.

Sortant de derrière un poster,
(C)
Espérant que la vie ne fût si longue.

Chorus 3

C   Em   Am
Ah,—— we fade to grey, fade to grey.
C   Em   Am
Ah,—— we fade to grey, fade to grey.

Verse 3

Dm   F
Feel the rain like an English summer,
                        Am
Hear the notes from a distant song.
Dm   F
Stepping out from a back drop poster,
                        Am
Wishing life wouldn't be so long.   *(Devenions gris.)*

Chorus 4

C   Em   Am
Ah,—— we fade to grey, fade to grey.
C   Em   Am
Ah,—— we fade to grey, fade to grey.
C   Em   Am
Ah,—— we fade to grey, fade to grey. *(Devenions gris.)*
C   Em   Am
Ah,—— we fade to grey, fade to grey. *(Devenions gris.)*
    C   Em   Am
‖: Ah,—— we fade to grey, fade to grey.
C   Em   Am
Ah,—— we fade to grey, fade to grey. *(Devenions gris.)* :‖

(Repeat to Fade)

TOM WAITS: Blue Valentines

Words & Music by
Tom Waits

Intro | Dm9 | E9 | Dm9 | E9 | Dm9 | E9 ‖

Verse 1

        Dm7 **E9**
She sends me, blue valentines,

  Dm7   **E9**
All the way from Phila - delphia.

  Dm7   **E9**
To mark the anni - versary,

  Am7   **A7**
Of someone that I used to be.

   Dm7   **E9**
And it feels just like there's a warrant,

Am7   **A7**
Out for my arrest.

       Dm7   **E9**   **Am7** **A7**
Baby, you got me checkin' in my rearview mirror,

      Dm7   **E9**
That's why I'm always on the run.

     Am7
That's why I changed my name,

   B7   **E9**
And I didn't think you'd ever find me here.

Verse 2

      Dm⁷ **E⁹**
To send me, blue   valentines,

    Dm⁷   **E⁹**
Like half forgotten dreams.

    Dm⁷   **E⁹**
Like a pebble in my shoe,

   Am⁷   **A⁷**
As I walk these streets.

      Dm⁷   **E⁹**
And the ghost of your memory,

     Am⁷   **A⁷**
Baby, is the thistle in the kiss.

    Dm⁷   **E⁹**   **Am⁷** **A⁷**
It's the burgler that can break a roses neck.

    Dm⁷   **E⁹**
It's the tattooed broken promise

    Am⁷
I gotta hide beneath my sleeve.

     B⁷   **E⁹**
I'm gonna see you every time I turn my back.

Solo

| Dm⁷ E⁹ | Dm⁷ E⁹ | Dm⁷ E⁹ | Am⁷ A⁷ |

| Dm⁷ E⁹ | Am⁷ A⁷ | Dm⁷ E⁹ | Am⁷ A⁷ |

| Dm⁷ E⁹ | Am⁷ | B⁷ | E⁹ ‖

Verse 3

      Dm⁷ **E⁹**
She sends me blue   valentines,

    Dm⁷   **E⁹**
Though I try to re - main at large.

     Dm⁷   **E⁹**
They're in - sisting that our love,

     Am⁷   **A⁷**
Must have a eulogy.

     Dm⁷   **E⁹**
Why do I save all this madness,

      Am⁷   **A⁷**
Here in the nightstand drawer.

    Dm⁷   **E⁹**
There to haunt upon my shoulders,

    Am⁷ **A⁷**
Baby I know.

    Dm⁷   **E⁹**   **Am⁷**
I'd be luckier to walk around everywhere I go.

    B⁷
With a blind and broken heart,

        E⁹
That sleeps be - neath my lapel.

Verse 4

        Dm7 **E9**
Instead, these blue valentines,

    Dm7   **E9**
To remind me of my cardinal sin.

     Dm7   **E9**
I can never wash the guilt,

         Am7   **A7**
Or get these bloodstains off my hands.

     Dm7   **E9**
And it takes a whole lotta whiskey,

  Am7   **A7**
To make this nightmares go away.

     Dm9   **E9**   **Am7** **A7**
And I cut my bleedin' heart out every night.

        Dm7   **E9**   **Am7**
And I'm gonna die a little more on each St. Valentines day.

      B7   **E9**
Don't you remember that I promised I would write you,

    Dm7 **E9**
These blue valentines,

Dm9 **E9**   **Dm9** **E9**   **Am9**
Blue valentines, blue valen - tines.

WIRE: Outdoor Miner

Words & Music by
Colin Newman & Graham Lewis

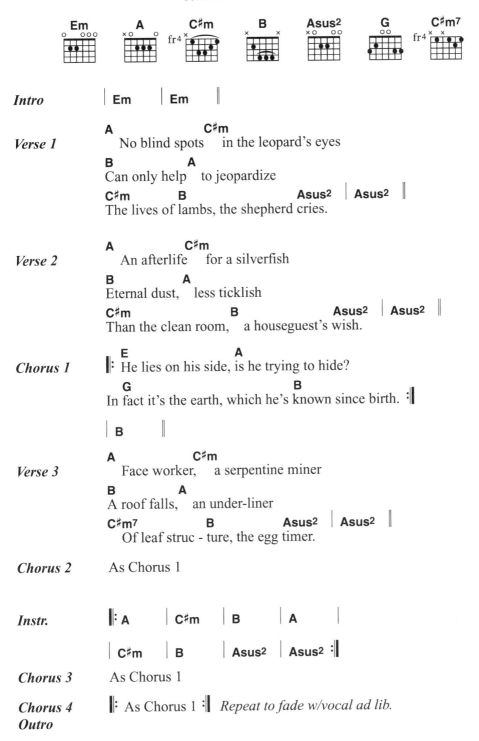

Intro | Em | Em ‖

Verse 1
    A   **C♯m**
   No blind spots   in the leopard's eyes
B   **A**
Can only help   to jeopardize
C♯m   **B**   **Asus2** | **Asus2** ‖
The lives of lambs, the shepherd cries.

Verse 2
    A   **C♯m**
   An afterlife   for a silverfish
B   **A**
Eternal dust,   less ticklish
C♯m   **B**   **Asus2** | **Asus2** ‖
Than the clean room,   a houseguest's wish.

Chorus 1
    E   **A**
‖: He lies on his side, is he trying to hide?
   G   **B**
In fact it's the earth, which he's known since birth. :‖

| B | ‖

Verse 3
    A   **C♯m**
   Face worker,   a serpentine miner
B   **A**
A roof falls,   an under-liner
C♯m7   **B**   **Asus2** | **Asus2** ‖
   Of leaf struc - ture, the egg timer.

Chorus 2   As Chorus 1

Instr.   ‖: A | C♯m | B | A |
| C♯m | B | Asus2 | Asus2 :‖

Chorus 3   As Chorus 1

Chorus 4
Outro   ‖: As Chorus 1 :‖ *Repeat to fade w/vocal ad lib.*

X: Los Angeles

Words & Music by
Exene Carvenka & John Doe

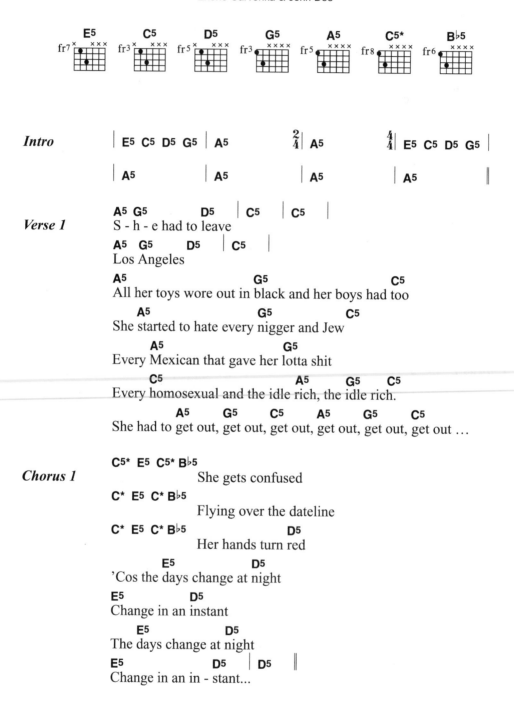

Intro

| E5 C5 D5 G5 | A5   2/4 A5   4/4 E5 C5 D5 G5 |

| A5 | A5 | A5 | A5 |

Verse 1

A5 G5   D5 | C5 | C5 |
S - h - e had to leave

A5   G5   D5 | C5 |
Los Angeles

A5   G5   C5
All her toys wore out in black and her boys had too

     A5   G5   C5
She started to hate every nigger and Jew

      A5   G5
Every Mexican that gave her lotta shit

     C5   A5   G5   C5
Every homosexual and the idle rich, the idle rich.

      A5   G5   C5   A5   G5   C5
She had to get out, get out, get out, get out, get out, get out …

Chorus 1

C5* E5 C5* B♭5
            She gets confused

C* E5 C* B♭5
           Flying over the dateline

C* E5 C* B♭5   D5
           Her hands turn red

        E5   D5
'Cos the days change at night

E5   D5
Change in an instant

      E5   D5
The days change at night

E5   D5 | D5 ‖
Change in an in - stant...

Link 1

| E5 C5 D5 G5 | A5 | A5 | A5 | A5 ‖

Verse 2

A5 G5   D5 | C5 | C5 |
S - h - e had to leave

A5 G5   D5 | C5 |
Los Angeles

           A5   G5
She found it hard to say goodbye

         C5
To her own best friend,

        A5   G5   C5
She bought a clock on Hollywood Boulevard the day she left

A5   G5 C5 A5   G5 C5
It felt sad, it felt sad, it felt sad

          A5   G5   C5   A5   G5   C5
She had to get out, get out, get out, get out, get out, get outÉ.

Chorus 2

C5* E5 C5* B♭5
        She gets confused

C5* E5 C5* B♭5
        Flying over the dateline

C5* E5 C5* B♭5   D5
        Her hands turn red

     E5   D5
'Cos the days change at night

E5   D5
Change in an instant

   E5   D5
The days change at night

E5   D5
Change in an in - stant

   E5   D5
The days change at night

E5   D5 | D5 | E5 C5 D5 G5 | A5 ‖
Change in an in - stant.

YEAH YEAH YEAHS: Pin

Words & Music by
Karen O, Nicholas Zinner & Brian Chase

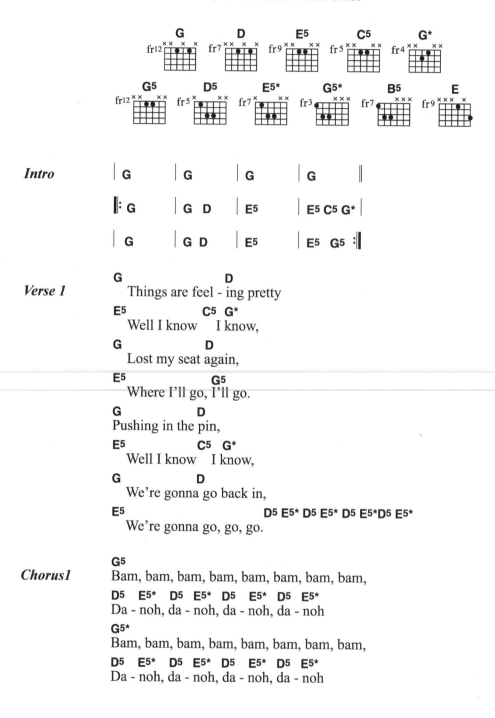

Intro | G | G | G | G ‖

‖: G | G D | E5 | E5 C5 G* |

| G | G D | E5 | E5 G5 :‖

Verse 1

G   D
Things are feel - ing pretty

E5   C5 G*
Well I know   I know,

G   D
Lost my seat again,

E5   G5
Where I'll go, I'll go.

G   D
Pushing in the pin,

E5   C5 G*
Well I know   I know,

G   D
We're gonna go back in,

E5   D5 E5* D5 E5* D5 E5*D5 E5*
We're gonna go, go, go.

Chorus1

G5
Bam, bam, bam, bam, bam, bam, bam, bam,

D5   E5*   D5   E5*   D5   E5*   D5   E5*
Da - noh, da - noh, da - noh, da - noh

G5*
Bam, bam, bam, bam, bam, bam, bam, bam,

D5   E5*   D5   E5*   D5   E5*   D5   E5*
Da - noh, da - noh, da - noh, da - noh

cont.

G5*
Bam, bam, bam, bam, bam, bam, bam, bam, bam,

D5   E5*   D5   E5*   D5   E5*   D5   E5*
Da - noh, da - noh, da - noh, da - noh

G5*   **D5**   **B5**
Bam, bam, bam, bam, bam, bam, bam, bam, bam!

Instr. | **B5** | **B5** | **B5** | **B5** | **B5** | **B5** |

| **B5** | **B5** | **E5** | **E5** | **E** | **E**   ‖

Verse 2

G   **D**
I like to sleep with them,

E5   **C5**   **G***
   Pushing in the pin

G   **D**
I like to sleep with them,

E5   **G5**
   Well I know I know,

G   **D**
   We're gonna go back in,

E5   **C5**   **G***
   We're gonna go,   go, go

G   **D**
   We're gonna go back in,

E5   **D5 E5* D5 E5* D5 E5*D5 E5***
   We're gonna go, go, go.

Chorus 2

G5
Bam, bam, bam, bam, bam, bam, bam, bam,

D5   E5*   D5   E5*   D5   E5*   D5   E5*
Da - noh, da - noh, da - noh, da - noh

G5*
Bam, bam, bam, bam, bam, bam, bam, bam,

D5   E5*   D5   E5*   D5   E5*   D5   E5*
Da - noh, da - noh, da - noh, da - noh

G5*
Bam, bam, bam, bam, bam, bam, bam, bam, bam,

D5   E5*   D5   E5*   D5   E5*   D5   E5*
Da - noh, da - noh, da - noh, da - noh

G5*   **D5**   **E**   **E5***
Bam, bam, bam, bam, bam, bam, bam, bam, bam!

205

FRANK ZAPPA:
Take Your Clothes Off When You Dance

Words & Music by
Frank Zappa

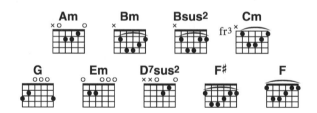

Verse 1

Am
There will come a time when everybody,

Bm
Who is lonely will be free,

Bsus2
To sing and dance and love.

Am
There will come a time when every evil,

Bm
That we know will be an evil,

Bsus2
That we can rise above.

Chorus 1

Cm
Who cares if hair is long or short,

Or sprayed or partly grayed,

G   **Em**
We know that hair ain't where it's at.

Am
There will come a time when you won't

D7sus2   **G**
Even be ashamed if you are fat.

F#   **F**   **Em**
Wah, wah, wah, wah.

Solo   ‖: **Am** | **Am** | **Bm** | **Bm Bsus²** :‖

La la la la *etc.* (*1º only*)

| **Cm** | **Cm** | **G** | **Em** |

Diddle-liddle-ly *etc.*

| **Am** | **D7sus²** | **G** |

    F# **F**   **Em**

Wah, wah, wah, wah.

Am

Verse 2   There will come a time when everybody,

    Bm

Who is lonely will be free,

        Bsus²

To sing and dance and love.

Am

There will come a time when every evil,

    Bm

That we know will be an evil,

    Bsus²

That we can rise above.

    Cm

Chorus 2   Who cares if you're so poor you can't afford,

       G   **Em**

To buy a pair of mod a-go-go stretch-elastic pants?

Am   **D7sus²**

There will come a time when you can even,

       G

Take your clothes off when you dance.

Relative Tuning

The guitar can be tuned with the aid of pitch pipes or dedicated electronic guitar tuners which are available through your local music dealer. If you do not have a tuning device, you can use relative tuning. Estimate the pitch of the 6th string as near as possible to E or at least a comfortable pitch (not too high, as you might break other strings in tuning up). Then, while checking the various positions on the diagram, place a finger from your left hand on the:

5th fret of the E or 6th string and **tune the open A** (or 5th string) to the note (A)

5th fret of the A or 5th string and **tune the open D** (or 4th string) to the note (D)

5th fret of the D or 4th string and **tune the open G** (or 3rd string) to the note (G)

4th fret of the G or 3rd string and **tune the open B** (or 2nd string) to the note (B)

5th fret of the B or 2nd string and **tune the open E** (or 1st string) to the note (E)

E	A	D	G	B	E
or	or	or	or	or	or
6th	5th	4th	3rd	2nd	1st

Head

Nut

1st Fret

2nd Fret

3rd Fret

4th Fret

5th Fret

Reading Chord Boxes

Chord boxes are diagrams of the guitar neck viewed head upwards, face on as illustrated. The top horizontal line is the nut, unless a higher fret number is indicated, the others are the frets.

The vertical lines are the strings, starting from E (or 6th) on the left to E (or 1st) on the right.

The black dots indicate where to place your fingers.

Strings marked with an O are played open, not fretted. Strings marked with an X should not be played.

The curved bracket indicates a 'barre' - hold down the strings under the bracket with your first finger, using your other fingers to fret the remaining notes.

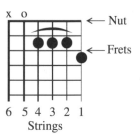

X O   ← Nut

← Frets

6 5 4 3 2 1
Strings

1 2 3 4 5 6 7 8 9